I Can't Complain

BOOKS BY ELINOR LIPMAN

Into Love and Out Again

Then She Found Me

The Way Men Act

Isabel's Bed

The Inn at Lake Devine

The Ladies' Man

The Dearly Departed

The Pursuit of Alice Thrift

My Latest Grievance

The Family Man

Tweet Land of Liberty: Irreverent Rhymes
from the Political Circus

The View from Penthouse B

I Can't Complain

I CAN'T COMPLAIN

(All Too) Personal Essays

Elinor Lipman

HOUGHTON MIFFLIN HARCOURT

BOSTON   NEW YORK

2013

www.hmhbooks.com

Library of Congress Cataloging-in-Publication Data is available.
ISBN 978-0-547-57620-6

Book design by Melissa Lotfy

Printed in the United States of America
DOC 10 9 8 7 6 5 4 3 2 1

For Benjamin Austin,
champion son

Contents

My Introduction and My Thanks   *ix*

Meet the Family

Julia's Child   3

The Funniest and the Favorite   8

How to Get Religion   16

Good Grudgekeeping   22

No Thank You, I Think   25

Sex Ed   33

The Rosy Glow of the Backward Glance   38

I Still Think, *Call Her*   42

A Tip of the Hat to the Old Block   46

My Soap Opera Journal   50

On Writing

Confessions of a Blurb Slut   57

No Outline? Is That Any Way to Write a Novel?   62

Which One Is He Again?   66

It Was a Dark and Stormy Nosh   72
Assignment: What Happens Next?   75
I Touch a Nerve   82
My Book the Movie   87
Your Authors' Anxieties: A Guide   91

Coupling Columns

Boy Meets Girl   99
May I Recommend . . .   102
I Want to Know   106
A Mister and Missus   110
Monsieur Clean   113
Ego Boundaries   117
I Married a Gourmet   121
I Sleep Around   125
The Best Man   129

Since Then

This Is for You   135
Watching the Masters by Myself   141
We ♥ New York   147
A Fine Nomance   150

My Introduction and My Thanks

I came late to the essay-writing genre, when various magazine and newspaper editors asked me to expound on a particular topic and I felt it was not only polite but also good deadline discipline to say yes. Before too long I discovered that which often starts out as duty can, a thousand words later, become an assignment I was awfully glad to have accepted.

I was inspired to write "How to Get Religion" after attending Julia Flora Reilly Golick's bat mitzvah in 1993 — so amazed and touched was I by every minute of that event. Its last line ("I pray you invite me to your wedding") came true, a most satisfying follow-up.

I must thank Laura Mathews of *Good Housekeeping,* who faithfully and regularly asks me for nonfiction, especially for her Blessings column. "Good Grudgekeeping" appeared there under (obviously!) a different title.

I am particularly grateful to the *Boston Globe* for not tiring of my byline. It was John Koch who gave someone at their magazine the idea to put me into a new Coupling column rotation, which resulted in "Boy Meets Girl," "May I Recommend . . . ," "I Want to Know," "A Mister and Missus," "Monsieur Clean," "Ego Boundaries," "I Married a Gourmet," "I Sleep Around," and "The Best Man," hence the 750-word uniformity.

"A Tip of the Hat to the Old Block" was a *Boston Globe* op-ed piece that ran on St. Patrick's Day 2008. Don MacGillis edited all of my op-ed pieces there, so lightly that I will always recognize him as a genius. "I Still Think, *Call Her*" ran in the *Boston Globe Magazine* on January 1, 2000, and "Assignment: What Happens Next?" in the *Boston Globe* as "Carrie Me Home: To Big or Not to Big?"

"Confessions of a Blurb Slut" appeared originally as "A Famous Author Says 'Swell! Loved It!'" in the *New York Times'* Writers on Writing column (their title — who'd say that about herself?) and was then reprinted in *Writers on Writing,* volume 2.

Ages ago, when Amazon.com sold only books, Kerry Fried asked me to write about my favorite novel. *The Many Loves of Dobie Gillis,* crazy-funny stories by Max Shulman, was my answer. Here, in "The Funniest and the Favorite," I've grafted to it part of an essay I wrote about my father for *Good Housekeeping,* "Father Knew Best."

"It Was a Dark and Stormy Nosh" was published in *Gourmet;* "I Touch a Nerve" in *Tablet Magazine;* "We ♥ New York" in *Guilt and Pleasure;* "My Book the Movie" on the Huffington Post; and "No Thank You, I Think" in *More* magazine.

"Julia's Child" was written for the anthology *What My Mother Gave Me: 31 Women Remember a Favorite Gift,* so thank you, Elizabeth Benedict, its editor, and Algonquin Books. In a different form, I wrote about my mother's condiment phobia in *Salon* ("Mayo Culpa").

"No Outline? Is That Any Way to Write a Novel?" first appeared on Borders' website. "Which One Is He Again?" was originally published in the *Washington Post*'s Book World section, as was "Your Authors' Anxieties: A Guide," for which I thank assigning editors, respectively, Marie Arana and Ron Charles, increasingly viral (in the best sense) book lover.

"This Is for You" originally appeared in the *New York Times'* Modern Love column as "Sweetest at the End." It remains one of my most gratifying publishing experiences, the gift that keeps on giving, for which I thank the column's editor, Daniel Jones.

"Watching the Masters by Myself" was originally published in the *Southampton Review* after its editor, Lou Ann Walker, asked me to contribute to the journal's issue on water. When I confessed I had nothing to say about water, she most kindly said, "Then write about anything you want."

"A Fine Nomance" is published here for the first time.

My son barely minds being publicly exposed in several of these essays and seems to think it goes with the territory. "The Rosy Glow of the Backward Glance" was originally published in *Child.* Even more embarrassing for him, "Sex Ed" appeared in the anthology *Dirty Words* (Bloomsbury, 2008). Thank you, Ben, over and over again.

As with everything I write, Mameve Medwed and Stacy Schiff were these essays' first readers and counselors. Thank you, dear friends. And thank you, Houghton Mifflin Harcourt, for letting me do this, with deep and fond thanks to Andrea Schulz, ideal editor.

And to Robert Austin, of blessed memory and star of the show.

MEET THE FAMILY

Julia's Child

THERE ARE SEVERAL things I know by heart, requiring no notes or source material, mostly along practical, gastronomic lines: you add a fistful of dried split green peas and a parsnip to the water that will become your chicken soup; you don't overbeat the milk and eggs lest your custard not set; and when making latkes, you always grate the onion before the potatoes so the glop doesn't turn pink.

I don't know what other daughters learned from their mothers, but mine was a purveyor of homely domestic tricks, imparted not with formal lessons but by osmosis, by example at the stove, in conversation, as dough was kneaded or liver chopped.

First, what you should know about Julia Lipman: She married late, at thirty-seven, but when asked by her daughters how old she was when she married answered twenty-three. She gave birth to me, the second child, six weeks before she turned forty-one. My birth certificate lists "mother's age" as thirty-four, and it wasn't a clerical error. She was dainty. She wore housedresses and aprons and never flats. Her bed slippers were mules, and her French twist required hairpins. She used Pond's cold cream on her face, Desert Flower lotion on her hands, and she didn't like drinking water out of mugs. She loved the Red Sox and mild-mannered British mysteries. She wore Estée Lauder perfume and never the colors red, pink, or purple. She did not drive a car, play tennis or golf, ride a bicycle, know how to swim, nor did I ever see her pitch, throw, or catch a ball. She was a queen of arts and crafts: a Brownie leader, a Lowell Girls Club fixture for twenty-five years; a knitter, sewer, wallpaperer, and gardener extraordinaire.

I wanted to be like my father, who was neither dainty nor fussy in any department. He scraped mold off leftovers and burnt crumbs off toast, while saying cheerfully, "Just doing my duty." I once heard him say, "Julia, what saves you is that slight streak of crudity running through you," meaning the occasional off-color remark she'd murmur that made them both laugh. I once found a petal-shaped piece of earring, sapphire-blue glass, in her dresser drawer, and asked her what it was. "Oh, it's from an earring I once had. Daddy stepped on it and broke it when we were dating," she told me. They had met in December and married in March, thirty-seven and thirty-nine years old. A stranger had once stopped her on the street, an older man who asked, "Why is it that someone with a complexion as beautiful as yours isn't married?"

I'm sure she said nothing; I'm sure she shrugged and said, "Oh, I don't know."

But my sister and I and our children, given the opportunity from within a time capsule, might have said to the gentleman, "It probably didn't hurt her skin one bit that she had a condiment phobia."

You see, before there were conspicuous vegans, before the era of lactose intolerance and sprue, when the description "picky eater" referred only to toddlers and children, my mother was famously finicky. I don't mean, *If someone served her a hamburger with ketchup, she'd scrape it off and eat it nearly uncontaminated.* What I mean is: If some unfortunate hostess put ketchup on the bun, my mother would push the offending plate away, unable to eat the accompanying potato chips, and ask for nothing else, her appetite ruined. And maybe eat a shirred egg when she got home. It was like our mother had a condition. She refused to taste anything that came from the grocery aisle displaying the vinegary and the savory, the relishes, the mustards, the pickles of any kind; the salad dressings, the barbecue sauces, the Tabascos, the Worcestershires or the A.1.'s. We didn't even own them. If a visiting relative needed some such lubricant or flavor enhancer, he knew not to ask.

Maybe there are worse things. I am no fan of ketchup. I eat my French fries plain, my fried clams without tartar sauce, and my Reubens without Russian dressing. My favorite mustard is the powdered kind, ground from the seed. Ditto my sister.

Now I feel bad. Our mother wanted us and loved us dearly. Her chicken and fish, her stews, her meatloaves, her lasagna and kugels and everything else were flavorful in their own, unadulterated way. Spices and herbs were fine. Lemon juice was a dear friend. She could cook and bake like Julia Child, undaunted by recipes calling for yeast or buttermilk or breast of veal. She made a lemon meringue pie that a food stylist would envy. She baked challah, Irish bread, cinnamon rolls, babka, Christmas stollen for neighbors. I have these recipes on index cards, half in her handwriting and half in mine. She sewed us beautiful clothes — prom dresses of piqué and velvet, and impossible little miniature outfits for our Ginny dolls.

By her standards, I was not a purist. I once looked up from my lunch of marinated leftover cooked vegetables and found her watching me with a puzzled look.

"What?" I asked.

She shook her head sadly. "I never thought a daughter of mine would like cold food so much."

Her children were food adventurers, she thought. She asked me why I needed to dribble balsamic vinegar on a fresh tomato when it was so delicious plain. I countered, "Do you butter your bread? Do you salt your tomato? It's like that, Ma." I know I scared her, once confiding that a squeeze of ketchup added just the right *je ne sais quoi* to my minestrone. And my college roommate's mother-in-law's recipe I make every time an occasion calls for a brisket? Ketchup again. But never when my mother was visiting. I never tricked her. I used some other tomato reduction. A daughter-hostess has to live with herself.

The gift of her prejudices is that almost everything I eat or contemplate eating, or scrape off a roll, reminds me of her. She is there when I eat leftovers cold and every time I dress a tomato. Whenever a buffet lunch serves only tuna, egg, chicken, and potato salads, I think, *All she could eat here would be a roll and a pat of butter.* I don't like to drink water from a mug unless I have to, and I've never tasted Thousand Island dressing.

Before she died in 1998, I visited her in the nursing home every day. As I was registering her upon admission, I said to the woman behind the desk, "Above all else, she cannot have condiments. Ever. Could you write this down, please: No mustard, no mayonnaise; no salads *made* with mayonnaise; no ketchup, pickles, relish, or piccalilli. No tartar sauce. No Miracle Whip, either. No salad dressing of any kind. Not even on the side."

Perhaps, in her diminished state, they could have tricked her. But, really, in light of what other grown children might be demanding for their parents, wasn't mine a small, benign request? The staff always said she was the sweetest person in the whole place. She'd lost her speech, so it was up to me to explain her religion. I had to make sure that this lucky institution observed the rules of Julia, and that no careless aide would let those poisons touch her lips.

JULIA LIPMAN'S SALAD DRESSING
Juice of a fresh lemon; salt, pepper, paprika to taste.

The Funniest and the Favorite

MY FATHER, AN AVID READER, loved books but didn't buy them, at least not retail. Our shelves held an odd collection of classics, cookbooks, humor, essays, and ancient history, all hardcovers (my father insisted that paperbacks were abridged), few written after World War II, none costing more than a quarter, and all from a dusty secondhand bookstore in Lowell, Massachusetts.

The store was not 84 Charing Cross Road; not a shop where one made discoveries of the rare book, eureka variety. But one day my father came home with something he'd picked especially for me.

"I think you'll like this writer, Max Shulman," he said.

"*The Many Loves of Dobie Gillis*?" I read from its turquoise spine. The word "novelization" hadn't been coined yet, but I sensed that these stories, having inspired the sitcom, would be . . . well, inane.

But then again, my father — the parent who didn't allow television on school nights — endorsed it. He liked only good books, and "good" usually meant funny. He worshipped Ring Lardner and, above all others, S. J. Perelman. "Give it a try," he said.

The introduction was written by Shulman himself: "The stories in this volume have appeared in *Good Housekeeping, Cosmopolitan,* the *Saturday Evening Post, Today's Woman,* and *American Magazine.* They are, therefore, clean and wholesome narratives, quite suitable for the parsonage library. (The publisher wishes me to announce that substantial discounts will be given to parsonage libraries . . . My publisher also wishes me to announce that he has left over from 1936 a large number of copies of *Meet Alf Landon* . . .")

Who is this wise guy? I wondered.

I read on: "Mean, small, captious, and niggling readers will notice certain discrepancies in the following stories," Shulman continued. "In some . . . Dobie Gillis is a freshman; in others he is a sophomore. In some he is majoring in law; in others he is majoring in journalism or chemistry or English or mechanical engineering or nothing at all . . . These tiny variations . . . to the intelligent, greathearted, truly American reader . . . will be matters of no consequence."

I loved that. Where was the pious introduction that prefaced all other books? I wanted to adopt this voice, to be clever and brash instead of meek and well-mannered; I wanted to make observations that were droll and offhand like Shulman's;

impolite and effortless. I turned to the first story and was rewarded immediately: "I cut in on them, laughing lightly at the resultant abrasions," Dobie says, after spotting Clothilde Ellingboe doing the "Airborne Samba" at the freshman prom.

That first story, "The Unlucky Winner," has, at its heart, a brilliant piece of faux-mannered bombast. Led astray by the party girl Clothilde, unable to meet a deadline, Dobie hands in "Thoughts of My Tranquil Hours," plagiarized from an ancient tome by Elmo Goodhue Pipgrass:

Who has not sat in the arbor of his country seat, his limbs composed, a basin of cheery russet apples at his side, his meerschaum filled with good shag; and listened to the wholesome bucolic sounds around him: the twitter of chimney swifts, the sweet piping of children at their games . . . the comfortable cackling of chickens, the braying of honest asses . . .

And on it goes, Mr. Shulman's ode to verbosity, for several hundred more words (". . . the beneficent gruels, the succulent tarts . . ."). "That was the first sentence, and the shortest one," Dobie adds dryly.

Wry, cynical, intelligent, irreverent — nothing is sacred on Shulman's campus. Professors are windbags and frustrated novelists. Fathers are tyrannical and stupid. Public servants are crooks. To be sure, Dobie is girl-crazy, and Mr. Shulman built each story around this predisposition. Pansy Hammer,

Lola Pfefferkorn, Clothilde Ellingboe, Thalia Menninger, and Poppy Herring—all meet Dobie's rather single-minded criterion for girlfriendhood: beauty of the shapely, creamy-skinned, retro variety. But why not?

What saves Dobie are his character flaws and his limitations—physical in some stories, intellectual in others. If he wins these beauty queens, it is by his wits; when he doesn't get the girl, it is because he plotted, annoyed, and failed. Romantic comedy needs obstacles to succeed, and Dobie has plenty: no money, no discipline, no muscles. (In "Everybody Loves My Baby," Dobie is competing with four Big Men on Campus for the hand of Helen Frith: "'I ran ninety-eight yards for a touchdown this afternoon,' said Davy. 'I shot twenty-four baskets last night,' said Ellis. 'I tied the Olympic record for the hammer throw yesterday,' said Bob. 'I pitched a no-hit game last summer,' said Georgie. I cleared my throat. 'I can float on my back,' I said.")

How wonderful that *The Many Loves of Dobie Gillis,* originally published in 1951, has come back into print. Its appearance belongs to the Eisenhower era, but its jokes are Seinfeldian. ("Her manners were exquisite. I had seen her at the Kozy Kampus Korner eating the specialty of the house—a sandwich that contained scraps of pot roast, gravy, chopped nuts and a dipper of sauerkraut—without even getting her fingers moist.")

It is absolutely essential—the laugh test—that I quote from "Boy Bites Man," from the tortured obituary written by journalism student Lola Pfefferkorn, "a figure that brought forth frequent cries of admiration from my slightly foam-flecked lips."

> No more will the flowers raise their multicolored heads and smile for Emmett T. Zoldin, upholsterer, of 476 Coolidge Ave. No more will the song of birds cheer his days. The winds will still blow and the rain will still fall upon the green earth, but Emmett T. Zoldin will not know. For yesterday as Emmett T. Zoldin was bent over a Swedish Modern chaise longue . . . the Angel of Death with merciful swiftness extinguished the flickering candle of his life. And no amount of tears from Yetta Zoldin, his widow, or from their son, Sam O. Zoldin, or from their daughter, Mrs. Arbutus Gottschalk, or from Emmett's brother Pyotor, still living in their native Finmark, will bring Emmett T. Zoldin back. And tomorrow when the Abide With Me Mortuary lays his mortal remains to rest in Sunnyvale Cemetery, it will be the end of Emmett T. Zoldin on this earth.
>
> Farewell, honest upholsterer!

As a reader, I appreciated this as the fully realized, polished gem that it is. But now, as a writer, I imagine Max Shulman (he described himself as "squat and moonfaced") choosing, then crossing out adjectives, searching in the first place for these names, these middle initials, this occupation. I hope when he typed, "Farewell, honest upholsterer!" he laughed aloud.

As my father did when he picked out his favorite passages

and read them to me. He liked to entertain his daughters when we were home sick, even when we were past the age of being read to. I can see him taking off his glasses to wipe away the tears of laughter over Lardner's "Alibi Ike" and his persevering through his own guffaws.

My first editor, Stacy Schiff, once asked me which books influenced my own writing, especially those of connected short stories. "Oh," I said. "Well, I love John Updike's Maples stories. And, of course, Grace Paley . . ." I hesitated then said, "But my all-time favorite is *The Many Loves of Dobie Gillis* by Max Shulman." There was the long pause of an English major and aggrieved image builder. "You might not want to say that in public," she advised. (Two books later I would name a character after Max Shulman: Martha Schiff-Shulman, best friend of the narrator in *The Way Men Act,* a tribute to the creator of Dobie Gillis, hyphenated for all time to the surname of the above editor.)

I felt exonerated when I read in Eric Lax's biography of Woody Allen that Max Shulman is Allen's favorite writer, and again when I read that Bob Newhart named Shulman, Robert Benchley, and James Thurber as his greatest influences.

Once best-selling and celebrated, Max Shulman died in 1988 at sixty-nine. In a *New York Times* obituary, James Barron quoted Shulman as saying he was good at humor because "life was bitter and I was not."

My father died three years later, a copy of S. J. Perelman's *Vinegar Puss* on his nightstand. Laughter in the sickbed was his prescription and is part of his legacy.

I was his baby, the second of two girls. As good and faultless a dad as he was, he was an even better audience. We four ate supper in the kitchen, my mother serving, my father presiding, Mr. Gusto in all matters. His own days were unfulfilling — he was a salesman with a Harvard degree, having graduated in the doomed year of 1929 — but career frustration was not something he talked about. Thus my sister and I had the mike at mealtime, and we could've been comedians on *The Ed Sullivan Show,* the degree to which our prattle seemed to entertain.

Decades later, at an event sponsored by the Women's National Book Association, I described my father's delight in his daughters' anecdotes. A fellow panelist turned to me and said for all to hear, "A study of successful women showed they all had one thing in common: fathers who listened to them."

My sister and I do solemnly believe — no, we insist — that each of us was, unquestionably, her father's favorite child, the shiniest apple of his eye. The argument goes like this: I was Daddy's favorite child. No, sorry, you're wrong. *I* was. We smile as we present the evidence of his devotion made visible. Finally, we agree to disagree, recognizing what a sweet and lucky argument ours is.

The author at five, and sister, Deborah, eight,
playing cards with Dad.

How to Get Religion

IN DECEMBER 1980, my friend Bobbie told me she was pregnant. She was thirty years old and single, then an underpaid lawyer for a state agency. She said her mind was made up. Her social life had not borne much fruit; she might never get married or conceive a convenient baby; she wanted this one. The father, Rick, was a nice enough man, newly divorced, seemingly embarrassed by Bobbie's pride of pregnancy (they were colleagues), and nervous about unwed fatherhood.

They dated, they argued, they attended Lamaze classes — at which Rick asked more questions than all the other partners combined. The commitment standoff, though mutual, was annoyingly modern, especially for those of us in Bobbie's camp. He was there for her, sort of; her friends and coworkers wanted something more, not that we could name it, but something like a declaration. When her baby turned out to be a healthy girl, we were thrilled; Bobbie's fond hopes for a daughter, for a true and reliable lifetime partner, had been realized.

Even with his long-stemmed red roses and his sterile gown, Rick looked lost and apologetic in Bobbie's hospital room as the maternal grandparents fussed and Bobbie the pioneer, lying gingerly on one side ("a hemorrhoid the size of a golf ball," she explained), regaled her childless visitors with birth stories. Bobbie and baby Julia were discharged and went home to Bobbie's apartment. Rick, as far as I could see, was peripheral. He held Julia and regarded her fondly in his own fashion, which is to say in the manner of a man who didn't have a way with babies.

But if Julia the infant didn't showcase Rick's talents, then Julia the child certainly did. For thirteen years he was, in the very best sense, a crazy father, a constant visitor and adorer, Julia's famously, embarrassingly devoted dad, the guy who drove the Newton-to-Sudbury round trip for every PTA meeting, sneaked into both visiting days at camp — meant for awkwardly divorced parents — and cut work to chaperone school trips.

Bobbie married a man named Dan in 1987, when Julia was six. Soon Bobbie and Dan begat Max. Even with a blue-ribbon stepfather on the scene, there was no displacing Rick, who nested in the family tree in varied and original ways. Rick went on *Max's* field trips and was authorized to pick him up at school. During Christmas vacations and on most weekend outings, Rick took both Julia and Max, whether it was to Disney World or Grandma's house or down the street for pizza. "That's the family," Rick explained. "You don't take one child and not the other."

In 1993, I attended Julia's bat mitzvah. Julia's mother and stepfather are Jewish. Rick is Irish Catholic from a devout family. Rick's sister, brother, and widowed mother came to Sudbury from New York. Another brother came from Philadelphia; a cousin flew in from Texas, an aunt from Alabama, and a great-aunt from New Mexico. Except for the sister who taught in Great Neck, New York, neither Rick nor his relatives had ever attended a bar or bat mitzvah before, or danced the hora, or, as Rick observed, "ever eaten challah bread." His relatives phoned him for advice from the moment the invitations arrived. What does one wear? Bring? Say? Does one genuflect upon entering a synagogue? Calling it a dress rehearsal, Rick went to a stranger's bat mitzvah and literally took notes.

On Julia's day, Rick sat proudly between Bobbie's mother and Max, whose adoration for Rick was everyone's best shot for peace and quiet. The rabbi of this Reform synagogue called Rick up to the *bima,* introducing him as Julia's dad, to read an *aliyah,* an honor, from her portion of the Torah. (Rick had offered to read in phonetic Hebrew, but it was decided to keep it in English for his relatives.) Julia gave a speech explaining that the themes of her Torah portion were forgiveness and appreciation. She said, "I must stop more often to give thanks that I grew up surrounded by an attentive and loving family.

My mom, my two dads, my brother, Max, and six wonderful grandparents made my childhood years very special."

Julia, I should add, is a beautiful girl, one of those genetic meldings that produce a sum greater than their contributing parts. After she finished chanting her portion of the Torah in a melodic and clear voice I credited to her Irish side, she smiled more broadly and rhymed, "Dad, you're our honorary Jew / Please come up and light candle number two." The ice was broken, and the crowd erupted. To applause and cheers, Rick scrambled forward, lit his candle, kissed Bobbie and Julia for all the world to see, and sat down. From there, Julia's couplets were a *This Is Your Life* roll call: her stepdad's parents ("Orlando's second most famous sight / Candle number three awaits your light"); Julia's squirming little brother (during her bat mitzvah speech, Julia said that if the Palestinians and the Israelis could make peace, she should be able to forgive Max, who'd destroyed everything she'd ever owned); and Rick's mother, tall and elegant in her black organdy dress and picture hat (the band played "When Irish Eyes Are Smiling").

Who could imagine such a day, with a peace and joy that were almost biblical — the stepfather dancing with the birth father's sister; Jews with Catholics, Republicans with Democrats, labor lawyers with management. Watching Julia with her school and camp friends, I searched for the embarrassment that an ordinary thirteen-year-old would exhibit at any deviation from the norm. But it wasn't there. Uncles, aunts, grandparents, total strangers claiming to be her mother's best friends accosted and kissed her, and every reminiscence evoked a smile.

There are more threads to the story, but who would believe them? Julia's stepfather, adopted as an infant forty-five years before, had just found his birth family after thirteen years of searching, and there they were, at my table, crying and beaming. The blended family was multiplying before my eyes, never more unified. The weather was perfect, and so was the star of the day in her dark French braid and her raspberry dress. Could a director have pulled this off? Could Hollywood have come up with three grandmothers named Sara, Yetta, and Kathleen?

Bobbie said she wouldn't have changed one thing about the day but was relieved when it was over. The two dads were depressed. They conferred from their respective offices, talking each other through the letdown. Rick took Julia to a Notre Dame football game soon afterward as a cure for the post–bat mitzvah blues.

I've been to a lot of bar and bat mitzvahs. No matter how many children are pronounced special, a blessing, a gift, I think of Julia, of her three-pronged family and her three-ring bat mitzvah, and I smile. Rick said the credit was all Bobbie's — that she was the straw that stirred the drink. Bobbie laughed and said, "I didn't know he was that poetic."

So, Rick — I apologize. Your marital reluctance was none of my business, and, besides, what did I know about you? You're a good man and a great father. I understand that you've since married that nice lawyer, Judy, I met at the reception, that Julia was a bridesmaid, Max the ring bearer, and that all parties approved. Congratulations, mazel tov, and best wishes.

Happy birthday, Julia. I'll never forget your bat mitzvah. I pray you invite me to your wedding.

Rick Reilly and stepdad Dan Leinweber
walking Julia down the aisle.

Good Grudgekeeping

UPON MEETING ME you'd find me pleasant, reasonable, and without question, nice; *nice* follows me wherever I go. But let me step aside and introduce the inner child, the one my father branded "a sensitive plant," who very much enjoys holding on to a good grudge.

The typical grudge-kindling offense is not weighty or even unforgivable. It's better defined as a blow to my pride. For example: The famous (famous in my immediate family) case of X whose daughter attended preschool with my son. Eleven years passed without incident. One day at the supermarket, she asked where my son was applying to college. Upon hearing his first choice, Columbia, she hooted, from the gut, "Hah!" followed by a sarcastic and derisive, "Gooood *luck!*"

She might as well have slapped me. Three months later, early acceptance in hand, I found a feeble excuse to phone her, and an even feebler excuse to steer the conversation toward my son.

"Has he heard?" she asked.

I told her the good news casually, as if naming a correspondence school without accreditation. She murmured a bland "congratulations" and changed the subject. Moral of that story: Don't expect the offender to remember her rudeness, and don't expect satisfaction.

I do keep trying, though, and persist in imagining a whole drama festival of conversations revisited. My grudges come in all sizes and flavors: there are the mild ones (failure to return calls, to RSVP, or to send a thank-you note for the hand-knit baby sweater with the hand-blown buttons); the ancient grudges (mean boys and idiot bosses); the vanquished grudges (wrote a letter, filed a grievance, called the mother); the consumer grudges (I've never returned to the chichi kitchen boutique whose snobby owner was so rude to Aunt Hattie, age eighty-eight, just because she asked if they carried Salad Shooters); the noble grudges (against bigots, anti-Semites, and bullies); the social grudges (rudeness, cluelessness, knowingly seating me at a terrible table at a reception); grudges once removed (against total strangers who have been mean to my friends either in person or via a book review); defunct grudges (against the dead, such as my first-grade teacher, who made the entire class take their seats when meek me accidentally bumped into a window, causing the shade to fly up during an indoor, rainy-day recess).

I've recently learned a Yiddish expression, *trepsverter*, literally "step words," meaning the perfect retort that you don't think of until you're walking away and down the stairs. My personal *trepsverter* is the tape in my head, always cued up, of dialogue I might have voiced if life were a soap opera, where good characters scold the bad characters, and the bad characters stand still long enough to hear it.

Real life rarely presents those opportunities. If I find myself in the company of someone who slighted me in, say, 1986, and I excavate the old insult, my conviction and my voice soon fade: this villain remembers neither the conversation, the context, nor me.

At the same time, I believe in accepting apologies. My shallower grievances dissolve immediately upon contact with a sincere "I'm sorry" or at the sight of a florist's van coming up my driveway. Am I impaired and soured by my grudge impulse and my grudge archives? I say no; it's human nature. And healthy. If one has feelings and frenemies, one should have grudges.

No Thank You, I Think

I WAS RAISED IN a family that embraced all invitations, especially the oversize, engraved variety requesting a formal RSVP and a new outfit. There was no discussion: Are we busy? Do we like these people? Is it worth the ten-hour round trip in a Rambler without a radio? Our weekends were gapingly free. When the relatives summoned us, we went.

It was a different era, the 1950s and '60s, and I don't believe either parent needed or kept a social calendar. They must have stepped out some evenings, because I do remember my mother's collection of clutch purses, her special-occasion Estée Lauder perfume, and the Krysiak girls as babysitters, but no scheduling conflict ever required us to send our regrets to the weddings, anniversary parties, bar mitzvahs, or milestone birthdays for which our presence was requested.

So it was an alien *no* that entered my family's consciousness in 1969 when my sister married her high school sweetheart, and his large circle of aunts and uncles began fêting the couple. One uncle-in-law-to-be, the baby in the clan, Uncle X, attended nothing. "Antisocial!" his siblings decried. I, the eighteen-year-old maid of honor, agreed. Who gets invited to an engagement barbecue in a Lowell, Massachusetts, backyard and doesn't show? *Inconsiderate black sheep,* I concurred.

Today I look back and marvel at the preponderance of relatives who *did* say yes. Uncle X most likely did what I do now: opened the invitation and performed the social algebra. Will this occasion, this sit-down salmon, this hard-to-find hall where career updates will be shouted over loud music, be fun or be a trial?

This is relatively new — my not responding with an automatic *yes.* Most influential in prompting me to write "not" between "will" and "attend" is the joint husband-and-wife fiftieth birthday party my husband and I went to a decade ago. The first clue that we should have made our excuses was the implication that the couple was adding a table, and we were the lucky beneficiaries of the expanded guest list — news imparted with the telephone invitation. Arriving at the luncheon, we picked up our place card announcing we were at table 1,000, or so it seemed. We took our seats in Siberia with our fellow also-rans. As we chatted, it became clear that our hosts had stuck with the literal conceit of *adding a table,* failing to integrate us into the general mix, because our perfectly pleasant tablemates barely knew the celebrants and seemed equally at sea. The rub here was that as we made our early escape, the hostess gushed that head tablers A, B, and C were such fans of my books, and over there at priority tables 2, 3, and 4 were former colleagues of Bob's, doctors with the same subspecialty. What a shame we had to leave early before we could circulate!

It was a turning point that became a mental Post-it, reminding me of the potential hazards out there in eventland.

As I confess to evaluating invitations with this combination of vanity and emotional stinginess, I must point out that many of my "No, thanks" represent contentment with my lot. When asked if I want to join friends for that play that got the rave review I failed to notice — $120 for the second balcony — I think, *But I could stay home, watch the "Project Runway" episode I taped on Wednesday, and be in bed with a book by ten.* I was never much of a party girl, nor did I marry Mr. Let's Go Out. Decades ago, a friend summed us up this way: Bob and I could not be relied on to attend both her Fourth of July cookout *and* troop to the Esplanade to hear the Boston Pops. It was very helpful to have this syndrome identified, because now I can say, unapologetically, "No, thanks. Dinner would be great, or a movie, but you know us: we're not good at doing two things in the same night."

It's not a tendency I'd have advertised at an earlier age — nonrestlessness, the "No, thanks," without more backing than lack of social ambition. Experience has identified and jelled another inclination, and that is honest self-evaluation about my dependability. For example, a phone call comes in from one of various national charities, asking not for my money but for my time. Will I address envelopes and deliver them to my neighbors on — the caller pauses, checks her list — Winterberry Lane? I used to say yes. Now I say, "I'm a very bad candidate for this. I'm not reliable. You'd send me the envelopes, and they would just sit in a pile of mail. Really, you could do much better."

And then there is the realm of the professional obligations. Requests fall into eight categories in authordom: Would I write a blurb/endorsement for an upcoming book? Would I read and evaluate a work in progress (a stranger's)? Would I read and evaluate a manuscript (a friend's)? Would I have a minute to describe how the entire publishing industry works and how one goes about getting an agent? Would I visit a book group that will be discussing one of my books the day after tomorrow? Will I do a reading at such-and-such bookstore? Will I speak to the inquirer's fundraiser/association/professional organization/PTA?

First, a disclaimer: I say yes a lot. And despite making the category of requests sound burdensome, I recognize every day how fortunate I am to be an author whom people publish and issue invitations to. Still, my first novel came out in 1990, so I've had a long time to sniff out what may be the less desirable venues, which is to say the readings where nobody comes and/or the attendees aren't — as my late mother would say — from the book buyers.

Take book groups: almost always a gratifying bunch. But I have learned to ask, "Would it be all right if I arrive after the, um, business items?" The same goes for the annual meeting of the Friends of any given Library. Again, experience has taught me that I am not always interested in last year's minutes, or this year's awards and thank-you gifts to the hardest-working cochairs, without whom . . . etc.; or the raffle of forty items donated by local merchants, followed by the presentation of flowers to the individuals who designed the invitations and made the cookies. I say this as no curmudgeon; in fact, as a fiction writer I am interested in life's ceremonies and awkward moments. But these occasions seat me not in the back row, where I could check my e-mail, but onstage, facing the audience, as I try to look fascinated or at least appreciative. Accordingly I inquire in advance, "Your event *begins* at seven? And what time, might I ask, would I actually be needed?"

The book group analog is this: I have found myself too often in a hostess's kitchen, amid fifteen strangers who all know one another, not just from discussing books once a month but from their children's school or the workplace or temple or church or the block. I consider myself outgoing, not uneasy with new people, but there's always a moment in these kitchens where hospitality circumvents me, and the prevailing conversational ethic appears to be, "Let's chat among ourselves and fine-tune our end-of-year potluck next month, lest the visiting author feel besieged."

I refill my coffee and murmur from time to time, "Shall we begin?" gesturing with my plate of bundt cake toward the circle of empty chairs. "Anyone?"

In the related realm of bookshop readings, declining an invitation has its penalties and its rewards. I don't want to be seen as a diva, and certainly want to be a trouper on behalf of my publisher and our mutual wares. More social algebra: Will I flop, or will I draw a crowd? What if I say no and I'm wrong? What if one hundred hardcover-buying readers attend, including reporters and movie producers? On the same book tour, May 2004, I was up against the final episode of *Friends* and the final episode of *Frasier,* the latter in Florida. Attendance: one fan, one cousin, and her date.

Can I ever really be sure what to accept and what to decline? Yes, if I've done the event in the past and know it's a dog. Take the pre-Christmas sale-a-thon where at least ten authors sit at tables with their old and new books, thereby encouraging customers to confuse the day with a crafts fair. They browse; they turn your book over, read the flap, compare the photo to the live person in front of them, smile weakly, then move on to the best-selling author two chairs down. The first time I attended, I consoled myself that there was a payoff, that the deli downstairs had corned beef and chopped liver and really good pickles. Second year, I brought my knitting, the same year I noticed that the paperbacks piled at my station had been signed by me at the previous year's author-a-thon. Third year, I declined, and I told the truth: too many authors, snow predicted, not enough customers.

I have a companion quirk to the saying of no: I must explain why I'm turning down an invitation, lest the potential host guess the truth, that I simply don't want to go. I always

RSVP with an excellent reason and ask the same in return, a little emoting and a lot of regret.

It's just that I expect a little effort, a convincing so-sorry-but-no along with the offer of future social intercourse. Such is a footnote in my self-styled book of etiquette — that one can infer from the turndown that it is a regrettable and unavoidable scheduling conflict and not a divorce. (This, I believe, is a vestige of my long-ago dating life, when there were *no*'s that meant never, and *no*'s that said, "It truly *is* father-daughter weekend, otherwise I'd love to, and after that I'm free for the rest of my life.")

What I've learned since 1990, the year of my first novel and coincidentally the year I turned forty, is that almost everyone accepts *no* with grace as if it's what he or she expected all along. The committee that recruits the talent for the conference moves down the list to the next author's name. The parents of the bride cheer when my turndown arrives, reducing their bottom line by one expensive rack of lamb and my share of champagne, wine, and fashion-forward canapés.

Further reinforcing my ducking of invitations is a response I often hear: "We didn't really think you could make it (across the country/on such short notice/on the day after Thanksgiving/since you don't know the bride or groom), but we thought we'd try just the same."

Off the hook, I send my present, regrets reiterated convincingly on the card. Later I hear about the deeply disappointed dentist couple slated for my table, whose teenage daughter is a writer, too!

I am tempted to say, "Whew. That was close. Nothing worse than a stage mother with a writing sample in her purse."

But I don't. A fiction writer's job, after all, is to spin tales and sound convincing.

"Greatly looking forward to next time," I reply.

Sex Ed

WHEN MY SON WAS nine years old, a family friend gave him *Why Do Our Bodies Stop Growing? Questions About Human Anatomy Answered by the Natural History Museum.* The illustrated book was a big hit, filled with the occasional half-goofy question like "Is it true that you can eat an apple standing on your head?" or "Is the skull one big bone?" On page 88, Ben found Question 132, the loaded one, which asked, "When do I stop being a child?" Beneath that were three paragraphs on puberty, including a sentence that got his attention: "Body changes in adolescence turn girls into young women who can have babies and boys into young men who can make women pregnant." That there was a connection between boys and babies had apparently never occurred to Ben. "How," he asked, incredulous, "do men make women pregnant?"

I, the evolved parent at child rearing's sacred crossroads, said, "Um. Let's go ask Daddy." And then, to prove it was science rather than cowardice, added, "He's a doctor."

Daddy was watching TV. I repeated Ben's question. My husband said in a voice I didn't hear very often — therapeutic, pedagogical, Fred Rogers — "Well . . . sure. I can answer that. Do you want to sit down?"

And truly, Planned Parenthood could have videotaped his presentation and distributed it: the penis, the vagina, the sperm, the egg — logically, calmly, no smirking. Ben listened and didn't interrupt. When Bob finished, Ben asked — not coyly but suspiciously — "How does the seed get in there? Remote control?"

Bob said no. The man puts his penis *into* the woman's vagina.

After a few moments of contemplation, Ben asked, "Do you have to get naked to do this?"

Bob said yes, you did.

"Did you and Mom get naked?"

Bob said, "I believe we did."

Our son stood up, exited the room, and yelled from the kitchen, "I'm never doing that."

We waited for his return and his follow-up questions. I said, "That was excellent. You couldn't have done better."

"We'll see," said Bob.

A few days later, at the kitchen table, Ben asked me as casually as he could, without looking up from his breakfast, "How do girls get pregnant?"

I said, "Ben! You remember! Daddy told you the whole story two nights ago."

His tone changed to one of weary tolerance, as if I were the one who needed the refresher. "Yeah, yeah, I know: the man takes a seed out of his tush, and the woman eats it."

Well, why not? It had its own charm, and I was learning something valuable: one shouldn't push the facts of life too early. I'd like to think I corrected his misapprehension on the spot, but I don't remember doing so. Nor do I remember his coming to us for more sex education.

School took the next step, a unit named Human Growth and Development, formerly known as Human Growth and Change, amended after someone (this was a lab school at Smith College) worried that the word "change" could traumatize. The boys and girls were separated for the classes; the boys got (I swear) Mr. Weiner, an experienced and married sixthgrade teacher. Fifth grade proved to be good timing, developmentally, because Ben would study his vocabulary list without snickering. Again, Bob did the quizzing. "Vulva?" I heard him ask evenly from the next room, to which Ben would answer, equally clinically, "The external genital organs of the female."

"Vas deferens?"

"The main duct that carries semen."

When Bob said, "Clitoris?" I took a step closer.

"Female organ of pleasure," our ten-year-old answered as matter-of-factly as if the topic were cotton gin and Eli Whitney. The vocabulary was in place, though not always the idiom: a few months later he reported to his father that he had seen two Smith students outside Davis Hall "doing foreplay."

I asked a friend with a daughter-classmate, "How was Human Growth and Development for the girls?"

"I had to straighten her out on something," she told me. The girls were shown a video about boys and erections. Someone or something sexy appeared in front of the actors, a row of teenage boys, camera aimed at their backs rather than their faces or their pants. As a result, the fifth-grade girls deduced that sexual stimuli caused boys to stand at attention: an erection was all in the shoulder blades.

Section two of Human Growth and Development was coed, a year later in the spring of sixth grade. I asked Ben how that was going, boys and girls together. It was fine, he said, his tone implying, *Why wouldn't it be?* I asked how his friend Nathaniel was coping with this mature subject matter, because I knew from Nathaniel's mother that he still believed in the tooth fairy and Santa Claus. Ben answered as if venting a class-wide scorn over Nathaniel's reproductive IQ. "Nathaniel! He didn't even know what PMS was!"

Seventh grade brought a new school and, midyear, a new unit called simply Health. Ben announced it at breakfast, sighing and saying, "We start Health today." A pause and a wry smile — I was his best audience and he knew it. "Third year in a row I learn about fallopian tubes."

He was an old hand. The teacher later told me that when Ben presented his special project on conjoined twins, featuring Chang and Eng, Barnum's famous act, he informed the class that both men had married. Pause . . . shake of the head, then: "Don't even *ask* about the honeymoon."

He's a grown-up now with his own place, a fruitful social

life, excellent hygiene, and good sense. I'd like to thank Bob and Mr. Weiner, the playground, his bunkmates at camp, the locker room, the Internet, and especially the Talking Transparent Woman at Boston's Museum of Science. It's an important job, and I couldn't have done it alone.

The Rosy Glow of the Backward Glance

RECENTLY MY PUBLISHER asked me to update my "about the author" paragraph for some promotional purpose. Instead of ending with the usual, "She and her husband live in Massachusetts and have one child," I added, "a son, Benjamin, who turned out great." I sat back and smiled. It seemed the right tribute at the right time, as Ben grinned at me from a newly framed college graduation photo.

That's where I sit now, on this side of my child's first twenty-two years, all of which replay in the most delightfully nostalgic fashion. Things that once seemed huge, worrisome, tiresome, burdensome, are now only footnotes in The Legend of the Reasonable Child.

The biggest travail that we've reduced to a fond memory is the fact that he didn't sleep through the night until he was six years old. It could have been worse; he might have carried on and cried inconsolably, when all he needed was the sight of me, a pat, a blanket retrieved — but how did we know he'd ever reform? Add to our interrupted sleep the public relations factor: the question on everyone's lips, beginning soon after his birth, was, "Does your baby sleep through the night yet?"

"Not quite," I answered — for the next seventy-two months.

As he approached one year, every passerby, every bum on the street, was a child development expert. "Walking yet?" they'd ask, as if my toddler had HAPPY FIRST BIRTHDAY, BEN! embroidered on his bib.

"Our pediatrician says they either walk or talk," I'd murmur, turning to my big, happy stroller passenger to prompt a sentence containing both a subject and a verb.

A partial list of early parental concerns and their outcomes includes: **Then:** Bad sleeper. **Now:** Age twenty-two years and ten months, sleeps through anything, naps anytime, any place, on any surface. **Then:** Crawled late, stood late, cruised late, walked at seventeen and a half months. **Now:** Walks, runs, skis black diamonds, drives. **Then:** Watched too much TV, played too much Nintendo. **2004:** Graduates from an Ivy League university. **Then:** Suffered acute anxiety when left with anyone but mother, father, grandparents. **2004:** Moves three thousand miles across the country, whistling all the way. **Then:** Shy. **Now:** Exceeds his five-hundred-minutes-per-month cell phone plan. **Then:** Addicted to breast milk, followed by cow's milk, chocolate milk, and juice not from concentrate, which is to say: *teeth at risk;* blamed myself for not promoting water as most delicious beverage. **To this day:** No cavities. **Then:** Not interested in toilet training. ("I not fwee yet," he would protest when we broached the subject.) **Today:**

Bathroom issues limited to wet towels on the floor and use of a fresh one for every shower. Toddler tolerance for dirty diapers is now seen as a prognostic of the easygoing, unflappable adult.

One of the great joys of the grown-up child is seeing how the essential him or her was always there. Baby versions of likes and dislikes, talents, interests, and personality traits come home to roost in fascinating ways. True then and true now: Ben had a keen interest in anything electronic, in the pushbuttons of telephones, remote controls, computer keyboards, calculators, VCRs; in dashboards, in menus, in dining out. Nothing bothered him that couldn't be cured by nursing or eating. Years passed. The only demerits levied against him in high school were meted out for leaving campus to get sushi. Every article he wrote for his college newspaper was a restaurant review.

I'm not pointing out in grandparently fashion that time flies, that your little ones grow up in the blink of an eye, so cherish every moment. You've heard that. This is me saying you have a lot to look forward to — not just the tuition-free, post-orthodontic, babysitterless side of parenthood, but the company it keeps: your grown-up child. My friends with small children have asked me, "What's it like when they no longer crawl into your lap? When the hugging and kissing get shrugged away? Don't you miss the baby?"

Yes, we do. My husband frequently gazes at baby pictures and says, "My boy was cute, wasn't he?"

But then the big boy calls, and the rosy glow changes direction to the here and now. Lovely surprises will await you, too: A big strapping guy! A witty friend! A voter! A licensed driver! A tech-support hotline! An adviser, a guide, a conscience.

A pride and joy.

I Still Think, Call Her

WHEN MY FATHER DIED in 1991, I coped by bringing my mother the hundred-plus miles closer to where I lived in western Massachusetts. Grief over the loss of my father worked its way into a relocation project: finding the right condo for my mother and talking her into moving away from the city where she'd lived for seventy-six years. Even as I told my son, then nine, that Papa Lou had died, I rushed to add, "But I think we can get Nana to move to Northampton, and you can see her whenever you want to." My mother was eighty-one. She left Lowell, her home since 1914, as if she were being transferred out of boot camp, with a grim obedience. She who didn't like change astonished my sister and me by getting the house spruced up, selling it, selling my father's car, and buying a condo in a Northampton retirement community. On moving day she announced, "I want to say something: I don't want this to change your life. You don't have to babysit me. I can take care of myself."

She loved Northampton, found it beautiful, even the modest houses on the side streets on the route between our respective homes. She volunteered at the community office once a week, baked poppy seed cake for all bake sales, and knitted beautiful pastel caps for the newborns at Cooley Dickinson Hospital. As elderly mothers go, she was undemanding.

But parents at a distance are a little more charming than they are close-up. Our first outing, a welcome of sorts, was a book group luncheon. I tried to be winning and entertaining so she could see me in action and be proud. I talked my heart out. She smiled and nodded regally from her chair at the head table, as befitting the mother of the local author. As soon as we got in my car, I asked, "So? What'd you think?"

She smiled, patted her own shoulder pads. "I think this suit was a very good choice for this event, don't you?"

She was eighty-one then, relatively strong, reasonably healthy, able to hear and stay up on her feet for the length of a mother-daughter shopping expedition. We picked out wallpaper, a couch, curtain fabric, new dishes, and, every May, Big Girl tomato plants and flats of maroon pansies. We went to see a lawyer and signed things that I knew, vaguely, we'd have to invoke someday, a power of attorney and a health proxy, formalizing her wishes that we, her daughters, make no heroic efforts to keep her alive. She had left her dour Lowell doctor behind and started seeing a family practice doctor in the country who found her witty and sharp, and pronounced her healthy — thereby making her so for many years. She found him adorable and reassuring, with his full beard and easy smile.

It was he who called me last March to say, "I think the most we can do is make her comfortable," and in the end, it was he who prescribed the morphine that calmed her and eased her way. She had suffered a stroke that left her with cortical blindness, but the day before she died, I was sure she could see me and my now teenage son, who'd said the night before, "Don't go to the nursing home without me tomorrow. Wake me up, okay?" I'd smiled and she'd returned it, a smile that said, "I'm in pain, and dying is the pits, so what are we two goofballs grinning at?" She never complained to the nurses, never talked back, never flinched. Everyone told me I had the nicest mother, the sweetest patient, their pet.

I still think, *Call Mom,* when good things happen, or when I feel the old tug of guilt — *Call her; is she okay?* The first time I made chicken soup after she died, and added a tablespoon of dried split peas, her trick, I stopped mid-stir because I realized it was a graduation of sorts. All the cooking, knitting, sewing, gardening, and even writing tips ("It's good, but do you think it's enough for a whole *novel?*" she asked once when I told her my latest idea) she dispensed in our forty-seven years together are complete. (Don't talk on the phone during an electrical storm; don't go out with wet hair; bananas before bed give you bad dreams; sleeping on your back gives you bad dreams; reading in the car makes you carsick; hair dye gives you cancer; raw potato takes the saltiness out of soup; don't overbeat the eggs when you make a custard; feed your tomatoes Epsom salts.)

I haven't been to the nursing home yet to pick up her

clothes or the framed picture of us, her daughters and their husbands, or to say goodbye to the nurses and nurses' aides who were so wonderful to her in the last months of her life. She's back in Lowell, next to my father, her parents, her sister. The rabbi at the graveside didn't know her but listened hard and got everything right — her personality, her unexpected courage when my father died, and her strength in the end — and he also made us smile. Nineteen ninety-nine was the year she would have turned ninety. She'd die if she knew I was telling you that. It's also the year in which my sister and I will have to find the words to chisel on her headstone. *Mom,* we could say. *Beloved mother and grandmother. Rest in peace. We only remember the good parts. How's Daddy? Call me.*

A Tip of the Hat to the Old Block

I'LL BE CAREFUL ON this St. Patrick's Day, mindful that sending a valentine to an entire clan of hyphenated Americans would reveal myself as sociologically backward. I won't generalize; instead, I'll narrow my focus to one subset of Irish-Americans, the residents of the Lowell neighborhood where I lived until I was twelve. What strikes me as remarkable from this distance is how my family and I were folded in, embraced, accepted as far back as the 1950s, despite our being the sole Jewish family for blocks around.

The 1950s were not a decade famous for open arms: No laws were on the books suggesting that religious animus was punishable by the courts. Pope John XXIII wouldn't until 1958 eliminate anti-Semitic pejoratives from prayers. New England hotels could advertise GENTILES ONLY or post signs that said NO DOGS OR JEWS.

My neighborhood was not the section of Lowell where mill

owners, doctors, and lawyers lived. Ours was one of starter homes, clotheslines, one-car garages; no backyard was big enough for three bases and a home plate. Yet here was my childhood: my sister and I never heard an unkind or exclusionary word leak from the homes that surrounded us. From the day Marie McGowan moved in across the street, pregnant with her third, she was my mother's best friend, confidante, and cofounder of the daily kaffeeklatsch.

With five daughters between them, hand-me-down dresses hopscotched between our two households. Because my mother was the best cook in the neighborhood, with a range from gefilte fish to spaghetti sauce, her Irish bread inevitably won the title of most delicious and most authentic. At Christmas, she made wreaths of cinnamon buns for the neighbors from a recipe handed down by my kosher grandmother. I still don't know why Father Shanley regularly joined us for corned beef and cabbage, but it might have been a preference for deli-style over rectory-style boiled meat.

Marge Gibson was the neighborhood's best seamstress, with my mother, a tailor's daughter, a keen audience. Thus one fashion memory more vivid than any my own childhood offers up is that of Suzanne Gibson in white dotted swiss, brought by for inspection on her way to her First Communion, her mother's creation more beautiful than any off the rack, especially on Suzanne, the adored baby in her family, with her blue eyes and dark finger curls.

Every summer night, weather permitting, my father walked

uphill to Eddie Reeney's veranda, where the neighborhood men smoked cigars in rocking chairs. My father marveled at Eddie's real-world skills; Eddie, in turn, treated my father, the English major and least mechanical man ever born ("Jets don't have propellers?!" he once proclaimed), with the studied patience of a shop teacher helping an armless student.

My father also revered the porch elder, white-haired Sam McElroy, a bachelor with a brogue, who lived with his two sisters from the old country. (I overheard my father tell my mother that it had not been easy for Sam growing up in Ireland: he was, my father confided, a Protestant.)

My sister, Debbie, and I dressed up for Easter, sans church, sans eggs, but kept our own council with respect to the Easter Bunny. Three years older than I, Debbie and her friends discussed religion just enough so that she came away accepting — not glumly, just a fact of life — that purgatory was the best she could hope for. St. Margaret's was our buddies' destination for church and catechism, but Temple Beth El, a closer walk, hosted the Brownies and Cub Scouts.

The McGowans, unannounced, came to my father's funeral — from some distance and thirty-nine years after we had left Cascade Avenue. And when my mother died, Marie, Pat (now Scanlon), and Carol (now Sullivan) were with us at a graveside service.

I should repeat: it's dangerous to characterize a whole group of people by their country of origin, or anything else. So today I'll keep it on a small scale, a salute to the McGowans, the

Gibsons, the Daileys, the Shanleys, the Mullens, the Cullens, the Crimminses, the Timminses, the Lemeres (Irish mother), the Reeneys, the Hogans, the Gallaghers, and the McElroys, whose backyards ran into the Lipmans', and whose embrace hasn't released us yet.

My Soap Opera Journal

1939 (well before I was born): My cousin Freda, age three, is asking for something in agitated fashion. Her mother doesn't understand what the toddler wants. Her aunt, my mother, translates: Turn on radio. It's time for *Portia Faces Life*.

1956–1959 (K–3): School gets out at noon. I eat lunch in front of the TV, first *The Big Brother Show* with Big Brother Bob Emery. Then my mother joins me for "her stories." Together we watch *The Guiding Light, Search for Tomorrow,* and *As the World Turns,* some only fifteen minutes long. The last is my favorite because of the Lowell family: I live in Lowell, Massachusetts, which seems uncanny. My father calls it "As the World Squirms."

1964–1968: Luckily, Title IX has not yet passed, so there are no sports teams for girls to keep me late at school. I rush home, cutting through Bruce Levine's yard every day to make it in time to watch my favorite soap, *The Doctors*. Maggie Fielding, MD, and chief of staff Matt Powers — will they ever *ever* realize that they are in love and made for each other? After that I watch the less cerebral *Another World* from its premiere episode. All I remember now is that Michael Ryan playing John Randolph needed a better-fitting pair of contact lenses and that I didn't like that poseur Rachel and always rooted for Jacqueline Courtney, who, as Alice Matthews, never stopped loving Steve Frame. I experience my first remote locations: St. Croix. Because I am not allowed to watch television on school nights, I squeeze in as much as possible before 5 P.M.

Real-life dinner conversation slips into soap opera updates for my working mother. My father says, unfailingly, "Who's Brock? Who's Nora? Who is Dennis Carrington?" My sister and I say, "They're on *The Doctors*. He's on *Another World*." He shakes his head slowly, eyes downcast, and says, "I can't believe my wife and daughters are discussing the lives of people who don't exist."

September 27, 1965–June 24, 1966: My sophomore year in high school, I add to my afternoon lineup the brand-new, soon-to-be-short-lived teenage surfer soap, *Never Too Young,* starring *Leave It to Beaver*'s Tony Dow. My father calls this one "Too Young to Know Any Better."

Spring 1968: I get into college anyway.

1969–1983: I suspend soap opera watching while in college and later into full-time employment. In fact, I am a little disdainful of my fellow students who congregate in the living room of Simmons Hall to watch *All My Children* and *General Hospital.* Who are Luke and Laura?

July 1975: I marry Robert Austin, newly minted MD. Unlike doctors on daytime drama, he never once encounters a patient suffering from amnesia.

1982: I give birth to my son.

1983: Twice a week a very nice young woman comes in the afternoon to babysit while I go to find a quiet place to write. She tells me, "I can come either before one P.M. or after two, but not in between." I guess this has to do with another job or lunch or a bus schedule. Finally, she confides that the one hour of *All My Children* is sacred. I stop asking, "How about coming at one thirty?"

Late 1983: I start watching *All My Children*. Favorite story line: star-crossed Nina and Cliff. Love the word "Glamorama" and later get my hair cut at a salon in Northampton, Massachusetts, named that as an homage.

Valentine's Day 1984: I hear from a friend who works in admissions at Harvard that many coworkers are avid *All My Children* fans. They brown-bag their lunches on this day and bring in a TV to watch Jenny and Greg's wedding as if it's a moon launch. *So much for the Ivy League,* I think. My other favorite firsthand report of Harvard meets *AMC:* an applicant comes in for an interview. The admissions officer, a guy even, asks him if there's anything interesting about himself. The boy says, "Well, it might sound silly, but my hometown is where the outdoor shots for a fictional town, Pine Valley, in a soap opera called *All My Children* are filmed." Thrilled and breathless, the admissions officer says, "Can you excuse me for a minute?" He leaves, tells a coworker, then returns to the interview after he composes himself.

August 1985: I attend my cousin Laura's wedding in Central Park. There, at the hot hors d'oeuvre table, I ask a fellow guest if his wife went to high school with Laura because she looks familiar. He asks modestly, "Do you watch a program called *All My Children*?" I gulp; try to look only mildly cognizant of such an entity. "Um — why?" I ask. "Because she plays a character named Midge." I love Midge, who plays a teenage sidekick in a minor role. He finds his wife and introduces her to me. I manage to say, hoping to sound like a thoughtful reviewer of the arts rather than a breathless fan, that she is a terrific actress with excellent comic timing. She is most gracious. After the wedding (cell phones haven't been invented) I call my friends Joan and Tammie, *AMC* watchers, from the hotel phone — very expensive — to tell them that I've met Midge. Silence. "Remember Midge?" I ask. Neither does.

Circa 1988: A friend flying in first class gets the sense that *AMC*'s James Mitchell/Palmer Cortlandt, unprovoked, is making a pass from the adjacent seat.

1996–1997: I switch channels from *All My Children* to watch CNN's coverage of the O. J. Simpson trial. I never return.

2003–the present: At three separate author events I meet three actors emeritus from *Ryan's Hope,* which I especially liked for its acknowledging the existence of Catholics and Jews. They are Faith Catlin, who played Faith Coleridge;

Louise Shaffer, who played (among many roles in other shows) the villain Rae Woodard; and Malachy McCourt, who played Kevin MacGuinness.

Faith, Louise, and I are Facebook friends. I've seen Louise's Emmy statuette (best supporting actress) in person. I learn that a mean character can be nothing like her offscreen persona. When I bake, it's often her excellent red velvet cake.

ON WRITING

Confessions of a Blurb Slut

IN THE SPRING of 1986 my editor sent bound galleys of my first book, a story collection, to six authors, soliciting endorsements (AKA blurbs) for the back of the jacket. The first turndown came from an extant Lost Generation novelist, apparently irked by a lofty editorial assertion. "If I wanted to read Dorothy Parker, I'd read Dorothy Parker," she grumbled.

"Nothing to worry about," my editor said.

Eventually kind words arrived from a short-story wunderkind who'd once shared a cubicle with my editor, from a novelist I'd met at a party, and from a writer published by Viking, which was also publishing me. My fondest hope, a comedy-of-manners top dog, didn't answer. On one hand, I understood. Wouldn't everyone want her anointment? On the other hand, I knew she had worked in publishing. How could a former solicitor of blurbs not send a collegial turndown? My heart didn't break, but it hardened. The final no arrived from a short-story starlet, pleading overwork but wishing "Ms. Lipman well." *What a mensch,* I thought. *What a gifted and sensitive soul.*

The first time an editor asked me for a blurb, I put my work aside and sat down with the manuscript. It stank. I wrote a full-page apology explaining how flattered I was, how disloyal I felt to my brother author and to my imprint, but that I couldn't lie. When the editor didn't respond, I called him. *Huh? Oh, that. Don't give it a second thought.* He certainly hadn't; he'd sent it to every living author on his list. And by the way, some rather big fish loved it.

My policy — no compromises and no dutiful blurbs — was codified after a minor moral dilemma. A prizewinning author, who had praised my first novel in private and my second in print, suggested I might have something kind to say about his new work. I called my editor for advice. She cut me off as soon as she heard the problem: that I hated most of it. "Don't do it," she said firmly. "He won't remember who was sent the book versus who came through. Never blurb something you don't like."

"I won't," I promised. (P.S. End of friendship.)

Nonfeasance is the norm in blurbing. Publishers expect little. Several galleys per month arrive at my door. I always open the envelope, and I always read the editor's letter. I like the personal, the flattering, the imploring: "In so many ways this book reminds me of yours, Ellie — . . ." (Heartwarming adjectives follow the dash.) Or, "I would be in your debt — more in your debt, that is, than I already am for having your wonderful books to enjoy, if only . . ." Am I truly this novelist's favorite author? Did her book group really do *The Inn at Lake Devine*? Maybe not, but what gratifying editorial unctuousness.

Cover-letter scholarship has made me didactic. When a dear friend's novel was being sent to her A-list, I stepped in to preach. The cover letters needed to be enlivened, personalized, grovelized. Mention the deserving author's worshipful admiration for the recipient of this letter. No form letters. No lifeless "I think you will agree that . . ."

Will I blurb a book because its editor implores me charmingly? No. Will I take a stab at it? Yes. When do I decide? I read until something stops me: Clunky sentences. No life. No story. Too much story. Too many italics. Too earnest or pretentious or writerly.

I generally give the promising stuff, the big-name stuff, and the friend of a friend's stuff a fifty-page trial. That's enough. If a few chapters don't set my matchmaking antennae aquiver, if I'm not thinking, *I can't wait to send this to _____. She'll love it. Maybe she'll blurb it, too,* I put it down.

A manila file folder labeled TO BLURB OR NOT? holds the galleys' cover letters, which I always mean to answer. Mostly I do; I e-mail the editor and make my excuse: "Thank you, but I'm judging a contest and therefore have cartons of novels to read over the next three months." "I'm on deadline." "I'm leaving soon for a book tour." And the truest of all, "My name is on so many books this upcoming season that I fear it will render those endorsements meaningless." (My computer stores this document under "blurb moratorium template.")

"I saw your name on a book," people say. "Did you really like it, or were you being nice?"

"I'm never nice," I answer. "I never write something out of obligation." The specter of the old Logrolling column in *Spy* magazine is a helpful tool. "Can't do it," I say. "He reviewed my third novel in the *Berkshire Eagle,* and we quoted it in the front matter."

I appreciate the sociology and transparency of blurbs: heads of MFA programs praising their darlings, editors turned novelists praising authors turned girlfriends. I will see a mentor thanked in the acknowledgments for his support, his faith, his in-law apartment. Then I turn to the back cover and see the acknowledgee declaring the book "huge, important, dazzling, incandescent."

I don't think I've ever bought a book specifically because of a blurb, but I've returned a few to the shelf because of an over-wrought rave from a pretentious jackass with whom I've had the misfortune to serve on a panel. Similarly, I've been put off by bombast, declaring this author the best of his generation, the heir apparent to . . . , the greatest living practitioner of . . .

Not that I haven't offered up a few overstatements in my day. I have gone on record predicting intimations of immortality and major prizes for books that were stillborn. On the other hand, I've been dropped from the jackets of second editions once the book hit the big time, and I've dismissed novels that Oprah went on to bless.

Modesty and reason make me wonder if anyone will notice "Elinor Lipman" on four books or eight or ten in one year anyway. Just when I think it's vainglorious to worry about overexposure, I receive something like reinforcement. "I saw your name on so-and-so's advance reader's copy," a bookseller will write me. "We're recommending it in our newsletter."

Perhaps I am too full of myself. When I feel a blurb coming on, I alert the editor that my seal of approval is on its way, as if it's an emergency; as if she's the answering service, and I am five centimeters dilated. Male editors are businesslike in their gratitude; female editors are more apt to be ebullient. One confided turning cartwheels in the corridors of Alfred A. Knopf. Can I believe them? I want to. And still better: hearing from the object of my admiration. This winter I received a handwritten note that brought tears to my eyes. "For as long as I live," an author wrote, "I will never forget that you went out of your way to help my first novel."

What's in it for me? Just that. If the system works, a shiny new hardcover will be turned over by a logical fan who thinks: *I like her. She loves this book. Therefore I'll love it, too.*

Word gets around in editorial circles, so blurb ubiquity begets more padded envelopes. I screen their contents because it's something I can do. In sports announcer parlance, I am giving back. Critics have been described as people who go into the street after battle and shoot the wounded. No blurb can be a bulletproof vest, but in my own experience it can put a square inch of Kevlar over a worried writer's heart.

No Outline? Is That Any
Way to Write a Novel?

IF I DIDN'T OCCASIONALLY leave my house and talk to
readers, I might not know that constructing a novel without
a blueprint is considered by many to be peculiar. The truth
reveals itself as I visit bookstores and book groups. "Any questions?" I ask at the end of a reading. Someone invariably asks,
"Do you know the ending of your books in advance, and do
you outline?" Most seem shocked when I say, "I know almost
nothing before I start. I just put one foot in front of the other."

Of course their astonishment is most gratifying. It implies
— and often a kind soul will say this out loud — that the story
seems tight, premeditated, and, my all-time favorite adjective,
seamless. Flannery O'Connor, I tell them, also wrote by the
seat of her pants, but she called herself an intuitive writer. *Intuitive.* I like that.

Then I bring up Edith Wharton, all-star emeritus on the
no-outline team. Legend has it that a completed manuscript

she submitted was lost in a fire at her publisher's. The editor asked her to rewrite it, saying, effectively, "How hard could it be since you already wrote it once?" Wharton replied, "I couldn't possibly rewrite it." When he asked why, she said, "Because I already know the ending."

More hands shoot up, and some of the audience members express relief. Either they are writers, too, and find the task of outlining a novel in advance too daunting, too time-consuming, too unappetizing. Or they are readers who want to believe that there's a little magic along the way, a muse pushing the figurative pen. I explain as best as I can how the muse has to be me. I am both writer and audience. I push ahead because I too want to know what's going to happen. The twists in the fictional road are what make the long journey fun. As Robert Frost famously said, "No surprise in the writer, no surprise in the reader."

People also ask about another authorial curiosity: they've heard that characters can get pushy and start calling the shots. At times I've felt something close to that, most notably with my second novel, *The Way Men Act*. I thought I was writing about Libby and Dennis, whose Main Street friendship was supposed to take a turn for the romantic. Yet when their paths crossed, nothing happened: no chemistry, no spark, no amorous advances.

As I began chapter four, my narrator, Melinda, stepped up with, "For the sake of clarification, I will say this one time that Dennis and I slept together before Libby moved back to

Harrow." I exhaled, greatly relieved, and thought, "So *that's* what's going on. Not only is this about Melinda and Dennis, but Melinda is an unreliable narrator." (P.S. Great fun to do an unreliable narrator.) Voices in my head? I see it this way: a new wrinkle suggests itself and prompts my fingers to type the words a nanosecond before I am fully conscious of having devoted some brain cells to the problem. Where the solution comes from, I don't know. To call it inspiration seems to forget the hours spent puzzling, revising, deleting.

The spark that ignited *My Latest Grievance* was, like most beginnings, a what-if. *What if a child didn't find out until she was a teenager that her mother had been married before?* No, make that her father, and make them . . . (need an occupation) . . . college professors. Why? I don't know. I'd claim "setting" except for the fact that I didn't lock that in until page 34. My narrator and her parents started out on a side street, off campus. But then the ex-wife and soon-to-be-troublemaker was barging into their lives as housemother on the campus where they taught. This created a point-of-view problem for me: how was my narrator, Frederica, going to observe the shenanigans on campus if she lived a couple of miles away? Pragmatic (as opposed to dreamlike magical) solution: move everyone to campus! Frederica not only lives in a dorm, too, but never lived anywhere else. Suddenly, I had my feet planted, and finally I knew what I was writing about: Frederica could be the Eloise of the campus, who sees and tells all (to quote a very kind critic) "with her mercilessly honest updates."

Do I plan to turn over a new leaf? To buy some index cards? To sketch a fictional family tree or create a montage of Post-it notes that track my plot? I suspect not. I start with one sentence. I write another. A character speaks, a door opens, and I find my way in.

Which One Is He Again?

SEVERAL YEARS AGO, at a reading in Kansas City, a member of the audience asked how I chose names for my characters. My first response was factual and dull: "I keep a phone book and *20,001 Names for Baby* on a shelf next to my computer." But then, a few minutes later, I found myself straying back to the subject. "I also keep my high school yearbook handy," I offered. "And my father's fiftieth-anniversary report, Harvard class of 1929, which I turn to when I need a throwback or a Brahmin name." Warming to the topic I confided, "Sometimes you name a character in order to reward a friend or punish an enemy." Another hand went up: which book and what's the dirt? Okay, I said. Anyone remember that sexual predator in *The Dearly Departed*? He has the same last name as the critic who gave a dear friend an ugly review in the *New York Times*.

The naming of characters suddenly seemed, on this rainy night in Kansas City, the most unsung part of how I get a story onto the page. After quoting as best as I could from memory what John Gardner once wrote, that to change a character's name from Jane to Cynthia is to feel the fictional ground shudder beneath her feet, I cited my own personal narrative aftershocks.

Before I had an Isabel for what turned out to be *Isabel's Bed,* I had a Dorothea, named after the meanest woman in an early writing workshop. I needed this character to be a hardhearted live-in boss to narrator Harriet Mahoney, hapless displaced ghostwriter. Something was missing, though. When Dorothea greeted Harriet at the door, I couldn't see her. Almost immediately, at war with my narrative intentions, this new character put an arm around Harriet's shoulders and led her to the kitchen, "like best friends heading out to recess," my fingers typed. I concluded that nomenclature was the problem. Real-life Dorothea had been sour, cold, superior. My fictional one was manifesting, against my wishes, a heart of gold. I turned to my local phone book and spotted "Isabel." I tried it. Soon, she was on the page. She was tall, she was buxom, she had vanilla-blond hair pulled back tightly from a florid, round face and knotted at her neck. I recognized her now — a dame who'd soon knock Harriet off the cover as my title character.

I made another misstep when I was a few chapters into *The Dearly Departed.* I didn't know much about the deceased of the title, except that I had to present her in flashback, and, as a headliner in the local amateur community theater, she was a small-town celebrity. My first reader said, "Um, your Frances? The late mother? She's a little familiar. If I hadn't known your own mom, I'd have guessed that she went through life with a turban on her head and a cigarette holder in her hand."

I said, "I know. I've made her a diva. I was afraid of that." The next morning I changed her name — Frances, for some reason, had felt hard-edged, pantsuited, manicured — to Margaret, a name I'd always found solid, dutiful, and, Princess Margaret notwithstanding, obliging. Without much in the way of authorial input, the mother I needed appeared. Her hair was short, brown, parted on the side, and held back with a barrette. Her face was sweet, her self-esteem was low, and her résumé was a few notches less professional. Unlike her last incarnation, she was not poised or worldly or aggressive. Because the opening sentence described this character's funeral, I needed a mother her daughter would mourn. Soon my omniscient narrator was saying about my newly mousy version, "Everyone knew Margaret. Everyone loved her."

When I teach, I now discuss the importance of names and their anachronistic potential. With undergraduates, I give them this exercise early on in a semester: It is 1965. Name your babysitters. (I'm looking for Diane, Susan, Linda, Donna. No Brittanys, no Samanthas, no Taylors.) Part two: It is 1925. List the officers of the high school graduating class. (I am going for Gladys, Ida, Hazel.) Recently, a student named her young, urban, sophisticated protagonist Estelle. No, I said. Uh-uh. The writer was fond of her choice and defended it. Yes, of course, I said, there may be a thirty-five-year-old Estelle who is all that you want your character to convey, but don't make your reader stop to ask herself, *Why Estelle?* Or Zelda or Hermione or Bertha. Don't, as Gardner pleads in *The Art of Fiction,* interrupt the vivid and continuous dream.

And then I tell them about the Kate factor. In any carton of manuscripts entered in a competition I am judging, the strong, young, sympathetic, attractive protagonists tend to be named Kate. Runner-up is Anne, Annie, Anna: old-fashioned yet modern, feminine yet strong. Kates and Annes can ride horses, drink, and change tires, but will still look beautiful in their understated wedding dresses, freckled shoulders gleaming at their beach nuptials. (Not unrelated: eighty percent of stories in these cartons, when citing some flora, choose bougainvillea, with its slightly Third-World, hacienda-ish connotation.)

Yes, my phone book has its uses, but I can't open it at random and point with eyes closed. An ethnic name is like the gun Chekhov talked about: if it's mounted on the wall in act one, it better be fired by act three. Names have subtext and identity. If your main characters are Kaplans, you've got yourself a Jewish novel, and if your hero is Smedley Winthrop III, you've given him a trust fund. Nomenclature done right contributes to characterization. When Wally Lamb named a baby Tyffanie in *I Know This Much Is True,* it worked; if we hadn't already known the IQ of Tyffanie's mother, it was there for the taking.

Names have a hard job to do: I try to make mine memorable enough to plant the character firmly in the reader's frontal lobe, but workmanlike and unselfconscious. Help the reader. Could the author please notice that Donald, Daniel, and David in the same novel are going to require a half second's mental calibration: *Which one is he again?* A Mr. Smith or Jones needs to note that he is burdened with or blessed by his common name. My editor tried to talk me out of naming a narrator Frederica. But look, I argued, she deals with that. Early on she says, "And there was the basic yet awful matter of my name, Frederica Hatch, due to the unfortunate coincidence of a maternal grandmother named Frieda, who died six weeks before I was born, and a favorite paternal great-uncle Frederic, who'd been a Freedom Rider at eighty."

You win, my editor said.

Dickens might argue that big-textured names let the characters introduce themselves (Rosa Bud, Bumble, Anne Chickenstalker, Lady Dedlock, Mr. Grimwig, Bradley Headstone, Krook, Charity Pecksniff, Chevy Slyme, M'Choakumchild), and thank you very much but whose "Scrooge" made its way into everyday usage and earned even the right to be lowercased?

Charity auctions have named a few of my characters. As I was writing my fifth novel, the PTA at my son's high school asked author John Katzenbach and me if we'd be willing to name a character in our next books after the two high bidders. We both said sure. The Katzenbach item, with its unstated bonus of an echo on the big screen, went first to furious bidding. Then the Lipman item: a friend at my table bid and was countered by a voice across the room. Back and forth, a few unheated rounds. Who's my winner? I asked when it was over. "He hasn't identified himself," said the woman collecting the money. A few weeks later, the wife of the high bidder squealed. It was John Katzenbach, winner on a mercy bid. (See *The Ladies' Man,* p. 197: the law firm of Dobbin, McLendon, Katzenbach, and Jessep.) Top honors for most creative use of an auctioned-off name goes to Anita Shreve, who was obliged to honor the high bid from a family with an unwieldy name. A few chapters into *A Wedding in December,* set at an inn in the Berkshires, Shreve discharges her obligation with a sign in the lobby announcing, "Karola-Jungbacker rehearsal dinner, Pierce Room, 7:00."

Particularly nice is the reader who detects meanings that escape the author. A book group member asked me if I'd deliberately given Dwight Willamee's sister Lorraine, in *Then She Found Me,* the name of a Teutonic goddess to underscore the tensions between the German-American family and the Jewish narrator. "Actually not," I replied. "I named Lorraine after Lorraine Loviglio, a dear coworker at my last job."

Recently, a lit major asked if I'd purposely nicknamed Conrad (*The Way Men Act*) "Con" because of the archaic meaning of that French vulgarism, i.e., "consolation of the lower parts," and its modern meaning (unprintable), which she found altogether fitting since Conrad meant nothing more to my narrator than the occasional horizontal encounter.

I wrote back, and I told the truth. "Dear Reader: I didn't know I knew, but perhaps I did."

It Was a Dark and Stormy Nosh

I WRITE NOVELS AND I cook dinner, and some days the edges blur. Like me, my characters know their way around a kitchen, and like my family, they are good eaters. Increasingly my plots thicken in restaurants, as waiters hover, and increasingly readers ask, "What's with the food in your books?"

My answer is, doesn't *everyone* characterize people by what they eat? Isn't it another descriptive tool, like a story's furniture or its clothes? It seems so, well . . . easy — the dialogue balloon next to a character's plate, an arrow pointing to his or her true self. For example: Let's say I want to sketch an ordinary Joe. Following the first law of writing fiction — showing rather than telling — I don't announce that Joe is unadventurous, prosaic, even dull, but I signal it by having him eat . . . what? (a) Sweetbreads on a bed of polenta? (b) Orange roughy? (c) Ramps? (d) Franks and beans? Or: A fictional man takes a seemingly appealing woman on a first date. He orders rotisserie chicken and garlic mashed potatoes (friendly, unpretentious, all-American yet bistro chic). Over her bottled water, the woman can't decide. She asks if the chef can make the risotto without fat, or leave the Gorgonzola out of the Gorgonzola vinaigrette. The reader recognizes the woman to be (a) on a diet; (b) difficult; (c) anorexic; (d) no fun; (e) all of the above.

After creating many characters who are unabashed eaters, finally I went all the way and made my heroine a chef. In *The Inn at Lake Devine* food owes its allegiance to two schools: Vermont cuisine circa 1964, and the Catskills (then or now). It was almost too easy: chicken croquettes, meatloaf surprise, turkey potpie, lettuce wedge, and baked stuffed sole, versus flanken, capon, blueberry blintzes, canned figs, and almond bark. Just as my narrator finds personal happiness in the enemy camp — in a matrimonial surf 'n' turf — so do Jewish and gentile cuisines coexist peacefully on her table: a smokehouse ham and Grand Marnier sweet potato soufflé one night, brisket and noodle kugel the next.

The first time I employed food as a narrative helpmate, I was writing my first novel, *Then She Found Me.* I needed a potluck contribution with airs, i.e., not a match with the other guests' four-grain bread and spiral-cut ham, and perhaps not to anyone else's liking. It was 1988, so I chose calamari vinaigrette — ambitious, daunting, and, I hoped, faintly ridiculous.

This reliance on talking food may be rooted in a pivotal social/gastronomic experience in my own life: At nineteen, I was brought to a young man's parents' home for dinner, at which his mother served calf's liver without apology. With so much serenity, in fact, that there was an otherworldliness to her composure. Did I need a degree in psychology to know my boyfriend's mother was (a) clueless; (b) opposed to her baby going steady; (c) passive-aggressive; (d) a few capers short of a canapé; (e) all of the above? [Reader: if you were writing this scene and wanted to intensify the culinary hostility, would you add to the plate (a) a baked potato; (b) white rice; (c) corn niblets; (d) beets and lima beans?]

Characters have to eat, don't they? Mine simply do it while you're watching. They make reservations, study menus, talk and cook, talk and eat, refill their wineglasses, linger over decaf. I'm at peace with this predilection because I find that every interaction with the stove, refrigerator, plate, and fork provides an opportunity to mine the telling detail, to make abstract notions concrete in a way I hope is a kind of shorthand.

Metaphors? Sort of. Blood, bones, lamb, variety meats (brains, guts, hearts) are entrées with symbolic heft. But I've found pleasure in telegraphing smaller coded messages: you know this person; you've dined with her or cooked for him. Happily, the supplies in this literary tool chest are limitless, and readers own the same ones. Tenderloin or tofu? Coffee or chamomile? Iceberg or arugula? If Anthelme Brillat-Savarin had been a novelist as well as a gastronome, he might have written, "Tell me what your characters eat, and I'll tell you how their story ends."

February 2004

Assignment: What Happens Next?

THE BOSTON GLOBE'S ART EDITOR, *whom I didn't know personally, phoned me to ask if I watched* Sex and the City.

I answered carefully — was this a survey? a culture IQ test? — "Why, yes, I do."

"We thought you might," he said, naming a wise-guy columnist who liked to tease me in print.

This editor was calling with an assignment: In six days the long-running show's much hoo-ha'd finale was airing. Would I write a piece in which I guessed how it would end?

I asked how long and for when.

"A thousand words? Twelve hundred? By Friday. But can you get me a draft earlier, like Wednesday, so we can get the artwork going?" Have I mentioned this was Monday? I said yes, okay, I thought I could do that.

It ran big and splashy the morning of the finale, just like this, without getting much right in the way of denouement predictions.

Last Sunday night, with my cable box tuned to HBO, I inhaled sharply and emitted a small sob of relief when Miranda the pragmatist leaned toward the repentant Mr. Big and said, "Go get our girl."

I hoped and believed that Carrie Bradshaw, lead best friend, would in this our final night together be granting my fondest TV wish: Forgive Big his inconstancy. Say yes. Come home.

Retro happy ending? Of course. But who are we anyway but fans of a fairy tale set in a glittering, kindhearted New York, "the magic isle of opportunity — not ironically but with the old Gershwin spirit," as Pauline Kael once wrote of *Saturday Night Fever*.

A few hours and many over-the-top outfits from now, we will know. Yet something nags, suggested by the chilling line Big delivered last week to the Charlotte-Miranda-Samantha jury: "You're the loves of her life. A guy's lucky to come in fourth."

I will be watching alone, nervously. Although my friends proposed gathering to experience the finale together, drink wine, and say goodbye, I want no distractions, no chatter, no knitting. I need my privacy. My husband, who not only hates the show but heckles it, is barred, unless he takes a vow of silence.

"Do your friends actually talk like that?" he asks.

No, they do not. Nor do they dress or party or sleep around in the manner of my best television friends. But therein lies the draw — the ticket to a distant land, the utterly unabashed, unapologetic girly-girlness of Carrie and Co., gorgeously overdressed for every occasion, in a paper-moon world sans parents or inhibitions or comfortable shoes.

I wasn't always a *Sex and the City* watcher. I missed the first season entirely, then chanced upon a few episodes in subsequent years. What finally reeled me in was narcissism. My own. The Corner Bookstore in New York, in what I now think of as Charlotte's neighborhood, had invited me to do a book signing. A crowd blocked my entry. The draw was not me, but *Sex and the City,* a crew filming in front of the store, whose windows were filled with piles of my hardcovers and nothing else.

Had I lucked into accidental product placement? Could the show's famously acquisitive consumers/fans do for *The Dearly Departed* what Carrie had done for Manolo Blahniks? It wasn't to be. I tuned in thereafter, religiously, hoping for a glimpse of my wares. Self-promotion, fruitless in the end, introduced me to four new friends.

It was the season of Charlotte's first wedding, the engagement of Carrie to a hunky cabinetmaker, and the return of a married man named Big. I was ignorant of where he came from or why he'd left. To fill in the gaps, I rented. Here was the Chrysler Building from day one. Here was Carrie talking directly to the camera, not with her trademark voiceovers, but something else, something alien and since dropped, a direct address of the audience. Here was Charlotte unattached, Miranda a few shades less redheaded. And here was a slightly gentler Samantha before naughty words screeched at high volume substituted for punch lines.

When the marathon ended, I acknowledged what I felt: membership in the sorority. I was no longer a fly on the wall, but the virtual fifth girlfriend at the luncheonette. DVD immersion had washed me onto their shore. I forgave their excesses, the painful leads to Carrie's columns, the rash weddings, and the rasher separations.

I still wince at many lines, and I don't love these women equally. Where is the overlap, the reason for my devotion? I share no niche with anyone on the show, not age, not marital status, not zip code or dress code. I've never worn a ball gown to a Chinese restaurant, never aspired to mile-high feathered mules; never even left my house wearing a black bra under a white shirt. Yet I put my knitting down when Carrie exits her brownstone in tulle and satin, or tangled in a crazy combination of inner- and outerwear. I lean in, take note, and wish for a replay. It is fashion as spectator sport, post–Title IX, full circle back to caricature couture, perhaps applicable on a small scale to my world — a white glove, a strap, a string of pearls.

Tonight I will watch *Sex and the City: A Farewell,* the pregame special, onward till 9:40 and then no more. Fortunately, I've discovered within me a high tolerance for *Sex and the City* reruns. On reexamination, I hear throwaway lines and nuances that I missed, or see that Charlotte's dress and sunglasses are invoking Audrey Hepburn as Holly Golightly.

There are rumors of a reunion, a special, a feature film. Until then I am steeling myself — and you must, too — for what I predict will actually happen tonight: the Russian and Mr.

Big will prove to be a story editor's tease. Carrie will choose Manhattan.

If I'm right, my longed-for happy-ending sellout will take a back seat to her city, her column, her bed-sit, her independence, her family of friends, her closet, her I-am-womanhood. And isn't that what we've worked toward in these six short years — ongoing eligibility up to and including promiscuity, and men as mere accessories?

I have considered the options. I understand that Aleksandr Petrovsky is the mature choice, an unexpectedly appealing diversion on the road posted with signs pointing to Big. At first I resented his intrusion, the deus ex machina arrival of this stable, rich, world-weary, unattached love interest. *How inorganic*, I thought. *How old.* But I came around. For four episodes I gave my blessing, defending him to myself against the ill wishes of Miranda and the doubts Carrie herself telegraphed to my couch. Younger friends of mine deemed him selfish, but I saw him as merely busy, distracted, his own man. Perhaps he was perfect: an artiste who loved her and could pay the Prada bills.

I hope I'm wrong. I haven't devoted all these hours to Carrie's welfare to see her settle for self-determination and freedom. I don't want to watch her flying home in coach, smiling her bittersweet smile, her head tilted against the portal window, Simon and Garfunkel singing, "So here's to you New York." In that scenario dear friends will be waiting at the airport — please, at least could Charlotte be pregnant? — no men except Stanny, with a pitcher of Cosmopolitans, balloons, puppies, the New York skyline. Gershwin. Credits will run much slower than usual. Begrudgingly I'll admit that any tighter closure would rule out sequels.

HBO will owe me a wedding with three bridesmaids in nonmatching dresses of blinding originality, and the most fabulous bridal gown of all time. I'll see it in a theater, instead of waiting for the DVD. I predict I will cry at the wedding, and I'll learn Big's given name. Ideally, I'll see it with three close, inseparable girlfriends, and then we'll grab a bite at a café, even if it's in a Massachusetts mall and not Manhattan. We'll gossip about our dates and lovers until one of us points out that we don't have any, and that Carrie, Miranda, Samantha, and Charlotte are only make-believe.

EPILOGUE

Four years later, I met Sarah Jessica Parker, star of the show, at the movie premiere of *Then She Found Me,* which featured her husband, Matthew Broderick. After spotting her across the room (Nobu 57, scene of the after-party), I darted in her direction but was headed off by someone from her past. (*Summer camp?* I remember thinking. *Or* Annie?) I didn't want to form a queue, especially because she was eating and because I didn't want to look as obsequious as I felt. But as I was leaving the restaurant, standing at the bottom of a long, wide stairway, wondering where my husband and son had gone, down came SJP alone, heading toward me in this empty space — "as if we were the only two people in the world," I have often described the sensation.

I introduced myself as the author of the book behind the movie, then rushed to say, in case I needed more bona fides, that years before, the *Boston Globe* had asked me to write about the finale of *Sex and the City* in advance of the last episode and to predict how it would end.

She listened graciously, patiently, adorably. Her dress was white with a big splashy blue print. I later learned it was from her new collection and cost $14.

I added, "I didn't get anything right. Well, one thing: that we would find out Big's real name."

Her already darling expression turned to one of astonishment at my prognostication. "No one guessed that!" she exclaimed.

I said, "I didn't mean I guessed his actual *name* — just that we'd find it out."

"Still," she said, with a firm shake of her blond head, "no one guessed that."

I told her I was looking forward to the upcoming *Sex and the City* movie.

Her expression changed, from earnestness to consternation. She said, with what felt like great sincerity, "Oh! I hope you like the choices we made."

I said, "I will. I know I will."

I Touch a Nerve

In the 1970s, writing for the *Massachusetts Teacher*, I helped sneak a headline into the magazine that later brought complaints. The one-paragraph item reported that the United Arab Emirates would be funding a Maryland school district. A coworker had submitted it with the gag headline, "Uh-oh. There Goes the School Hanukkah Festival." We were greatly amused — we underlings never got jokes into print — when it ran that way.

Letters arrived. Most fittingly, a member of the Arab Defense League wrote to say that our headline, with its assumption of Arab anti-Semitism, offended him, and he was, of course, exactly in the right. Less expected were two letters from Jewish readers. They complained not because they recognized an offense to their Arab brethren, but because we had made a joke in boldface type that — as best as I could interpret — had a Jewish . . . what? Word? Punch line? Invitation to discriminate? Suggestion of passivity?

It taught me this: people are touchy about words on the page and happy to tell you about it. I left education journalism for fiction and didn't hear too many complaints about the political content of my hardly political novels until I wrote my fourth, *The Inn at Lake Devine*. Where I've gone wrong, in the words of one letter writer, is the implied endorsement of "rampant intermarriage" in my books. I myself didn't know that intermarriage was the thesis of my novel, which begins with a thirteen-year-old narrator saying, "It was not complicated, and, as my mother pointed out, not even personal: They had a hotel; they didn't want Jews; we were Jews." Years before, when I sent that opening and a few pages more to my editor, she called and said, "This is it. This is your next novel." I said, "But it's all I have. I don't know if I can sustain it."

"You have to," she said.

I asked why.

"Because no one's ever written about anti-Semitism in comedic fashion," she answered.

Comedic to her, maybe, but no laughing matter to readers praying that their real-life daughter won't find, as my narrator did, love among the Lutherans. Random House published *The Inn at Lake Devine* in 1998 and Vintage in paperback a year later. Thus began my book group adventures among those whose hands shoot up to ask, "Don't you think you have a social responsibility to make Jews marry Jews?"

No, I do not. I have a social responsibility to tell an interesting tale. I explain: "This is *not* a story about a man and a woman who meet through a Jewish singles network." And might they at least agree that a fitting punishment for an anti-Semitic innkeeper is to lose her sons to Jews? Add to that the loss of her inn. Her empire. Like *Hamlet*!

I plead sociology: Mixed marriages to the left and right of me, long and successful ones, family, friends, neighbors. I grew up in a city with a large Catholic and Greek Orthodox population, which is to say I went to dances at the Transfiguration Church and to my senior prom with a boy named McCarthy. I married a Jew with the same degree of religiosity as my own, which is to say negligible. We raised our son in Northampton, Massachusetts, where the Unitarian Society delivers Rosh Hashanah, Yom Kippur, Easter, and election sermons. I try to explain my attitude — people should marry for love in this century — to the complainers (it's always women and it's always — don't write me — Jewish women), who want me to recant. I might throw in another example of the world I live in. I tell them that our son came home from school one day complaining, "I'm the *only* kid in third grade who celebrates *only* Hanukkah."

"It's true," I tell the hostile audience. "That happened. He actually was the only kid . . ." Et cetera. I ask if they don't see themselves as, well, let's be frank: prejudiced. No, they don't. Sometimes I add this, hoping to broaden the topic and get me off the hot seat: A novel about a Jewish family is a Jewish novel. (I name a few.) One cannot bring forth an American novel about the Everyman Family and name them the Shapiros unless the author is making a point. Ethnicity, religion, and race can't be dropped casually into a novel as if casting a television commercial with a multicultural aim.

At one particularly bracing night as keynote speaker for the Worcester, Massachusetts, Jewish Federation's annual banquet, a woman seated next to me at dinner announced that she found my portrayal of Jews in the Catskills more anti-Semitic than that of the anti-Semitic Vermont innkeeper. I gasped. I'd been taught that one is polite to the guests in one's house, and for that evening the Radisson was this federation board member's base of hospitality. Of course she had to repeat this later and louder at the Q and A in front of hundreds of women. I was flummoxed. A braver author might have snapped, "I don't defend the content of my books." I tried to get across what I used to ask my Hampshire College students, who grumbled when a female character under discussion tossed a salad or burped a baby. "In other words, you should follow the character into a voting booth, then judge the story by what lever he pulls?" No one used to back down in that workshop of the intensely politically correct, and no one gives an inch after I make my case for artistic freedom. "If one Jewish woman ever fell in love with one Lutheran man, are you saying I couldn't write their story? Can a novel be about Hitler? Are you offended by mysteries that involve murders? Are you mad at Tolstoy and Flaubert for those adulterers they dreamed up?" I quote as best as I can from memory (now from a document I wrote titled "Bring to Book Groups") what Flannery O'Connor once said, that "everybody approaches the novel according to his particular interest — the doctor looks for a disease, the minister looks for a sermon, the poor look for money . . . If they find what they want . . . then they judge the piece of fiction to be superior."

I've convinced no one, or so it seems. I have a responsibility, someone repeats. Our shrinking numbers . . .

Later, during the book signing, there's always someone who tells me that she converted to Judaism or married a gentile, and it's working out fine. The funny ones lean in to confide, "I loved this book. Thank you for coming. My husband married a shiksa: me."

I laugh. I open their copies to the title page and write gratefully, "To Mary Margaret (or Kathleen or Maureen or Christine), kind soul and brilliant critic, who restored my faith in my People."

My Book the Movie

DECADES AGO, ON AN unseasonably cold and rainy May morning, my phone rang, and it was Hollywood calling. "How would you feel on this miserable day to know that Sigourney Weaver loves your book?" this agent asked. She was talking about my first novel, *Then She Found Me,* and even though I surely knew that books could be turned into movies, I had no idea that mine had been circulated to producers. My husband and I threw an impromptu party to which I wore, aiming for Hollywood-tinged irony, a strapless dress, a rhinestone bracelet, and sunglasses.

It was 1989, and Sigourney was starring in *Ghostbusters II,* which I'd just seen with my six-year-old son. When I picked him up at school the day the deal was struck, I asked — expecting great excitement — "How would you feel if Sigourney Weaver wanted to make a movie out of Mummy's book?" He said two things, very cautiously. "You're not doing it for the money, are you?" and "Will it be PG so I can see it?"

Years passed. My six-year-old finished grammar school, high school, and college. I learned thirdhand that Helen Hunt, having just won an Academy Award for best actress, had taken over the project. (No one tells the author much directly.)

More time passed. Now working in Hollywood, my son saw an e-mail that suggested that *Then She Found Me* was close to getting made. ("Three great male roles," the talent agent's e-mail advised. "Hunt to star and direct.") A copy of the screenplay came my way.

At first glance I thought, *Huh? Who are these characters?* But within a few pages, I was in love. I sent an e-mail to Helen Hunt via her manager, praising the screenplay, a few sentences only, figuring she wouldn't answer. I told her at first I wondered what had happened to Dwight Willamee, the book's geeky-librarian romantic hero, but then I hardly cared. She wrote me back quickly and at length:

> All I've hoped for is that you feel April and Bernice [the book's main characters] are alive and well, and that the theme and heart of the novel is there ... I love Dwight. I imagine him sitting patiently for his turn to come to the screen. After years, I finally realized I had to find a magic sentence, a north star/theme for the movie that I felt deeply about and write toward that. Once I did, it became clear and I was able to start the work of putting aside a character that I LOVE, and trying to find the ones that help tell the story as I was beginning to imagine it on the screen.

How could I not love *that?* Yet before the movie even came out (in the U.S., May 2008), worried readers wrote me — not always politely, often highhandedly — about what they'd heard about Hollywood's apparent departure from my book. Each time I wrote back, saying variations on these themes:

1. I love the movie. Adore it. Have seen it five times and counting. It's smart, wry, and very touching. The book is the book, and the movie is its own entity. This I internalized early on when a wise friend told me, "Think of it as a movie based on characters *suggested by* the novel *Then She Found Me."*

2. This project took nineteen years from manuscript to big screen. I never thought I'd see this day, let alone experience the thrill of rattling off this cast: Helen Hunt, Bette Midler, Colin Firth, and Matthew Broderick. And hullo: Salman Rushdie as the ob-gyn and fertility specialist! And please appreciate the author-booster factor. It sold paperbacks with lovely stills of Bette Midler and Helen Hunt (in England, Helen and Colin) on the cover!

3. Helen (I call her Helen now) tried more faithful adaptations of the book. No takers.

4. I *would* mind the changes if I thought she was dumbing down the book. *Au contraire.* Helen and her team devoted ten years of their lives to getting this film made. She has said, in terms of that long road to greenlighting, "It was every version of no I've ever imagined."

Someone once asked James M. Cain (*The Postman Always Rings Twice, Mildred Pierce*), "How do you feel about what Hollywood did to your novels?" He pointed to his bookshelf and said, "Hollywood didn't do anything to my novels. They're all right here."

And back to my son: Tall and handsome, he came to the premiere in New York City in a Hugo Boss jacket we bought in a hurry that afternoon. I introduced him to Helen. He put his arm around my shoulders. "I hope you know you *made* my mother's decade," he said.

Your Authors' Anxieties:
A Guide

THANK YOU, BOOK LOVERS, for even *thinking* about devoting your Saturday, in whole or in part, to a lit fest! You'll be rewarded with stimulating, painless, and free fun. (Utterly up to you: the purchase of books that will help save our industry.) Not to be downplayed: the likelihood that persons to your left and to your right will be like-minded fellow readers of the opposite or same sex. Although no one promises that a literary festival is guaranteed fertile social ground, I once benefited from a feature in the *New York Times* titled "Readings As an Opportunity for Romance."

Although everything from your side of the podium will be clockwork and pure pleasure, we vain authors still worry about things that are out of our hands. Here, therefore, is a reader's guide to the baggage that may be fueling our silly, lit-fest anxiety:

THINGS THAT HAVE GONE WRONG IN THE PAST

1. The local newspaper prints the wrong day, time, or location for your event. Or leaves you out completely. You flop. This befuddlement will forever taint the city in your small mind.

2. The night and hour of your reading coincides with a critical playoff game or the final episode of the decade's most popular sitcom. In my case, in May 2004, both *Friends* and *Frasier.*

3. Always, no matter how scintillating you are or how noisy the microphone feedback and clanging radiator, there's a snoozer in the audience. He wakes up during the Q and A and asks a question you've just answered at length.

4. In the program, where the little bios are printed, you've supplied only the titles of your books and your hometown. Everyone else's bio has quoted rave reviews and employed phrases such as "critically acclaimed," "prize-winning," "Iowa Writers' Workshop," "best-selling," and "Guggenheim Fellowship." You remind yourself to add some adjectives and adverbs next time.

5. You stand poised, book in hand, smiling, waiting to be introduced, hoping the very recent review calling you a cross between Barbara Pym and Kurt Vonnegut has come to the introducer's attention. He or she approaches the mike and says, "You didn't come to hear me, so without further ado, please welcome X (mispronounced)."

6. You prepare; you read; you talk your heart out. You are interesting and even a little funny. You've considered what to wear: edgy earrings, interesting eyeglasses, lipstick a few shades louder than everyday. Then the very famous headliner gets up. He drones; he splits infinitives; he laughs at his own lines and doesn't know when to quit. You are so much better. You, up on stage, facing the audience, smile as if you are enjoying his performance, while all the time you're thinking, *Horse's ass.* Then the book-signing portion of the event begins. The patrons rush to line up in front of the bad famous writer, clutching several hardcover copies of his new book and whatever's available from his backlist. After signing your cousin's and a college classmate's purchase, you slink away.

   Worst reading I have endured: The fellow who said proudly, "I'm just going to open the book and read from whatever page falls open." He did, resulting in a lot of weather, derelict relatives, and bougainvillea. Tied for worst: The forty-five-minute reading in a hot barn by a poet who was drunk and gesticulating wildly.

7. Your books (the publisher's reason for having paid your airfare to get here) do not arrive in time to be bought, signed, and read. You hear that the distributor said they were not yet available/out of stock/out of print/backordered/due any minute. All lies. You are gracious because you are aware that not all authors are. Once, when I gently pointed out to the event coordinator that the

book I'd be reading from was out in paperback and I'd noticed she had only hardcovers there, she told me she knew that. She had a box of paperbacks, but she'd left it at home.

8. It's time for the Q and A, which usually isn't necessary. You want to kiss the person who breaks the ice, even if it's (recent question in San Francisco) this: "The coffee that the librarian in *Then She Found Me* brought to school in his thermos? Was it Peet's?" People ask who your favorite authors are and/or what books are currently on your night table. Several women in the audience write down your answers in little notebooks brought especially for this purpose and will later assign these to their book groups, possibly in lieu of your own.

LIES TO TELL AN AUTHOR WHO IS LOOKING FORLORN, UNLOVED, UNPURCHASED

1. "I've always meant to read your work. Everyone else I know has!"
2. "My book group is doing [title of novel you're not buying] in February. In fact, I'm going to be the facilitator. I love your website."
3. "I own every one of your books but didn't bring them today. I look forward to your next one."

GUIDELINES FOR AUTHORS

1. Never, ever read longer than twenty minutes. Fifteen is better. Ten minutes if there are more than two au-

thors on the docket. Practice reading in the privacy of your home using your microwave oven timer. Note that twenty pages does not equal twenty minutes; twenty pages, especially the too-beautiful kind, go on forever. Once, when a fellow author was up at the podium and going on endlessly, I wrote the word "time" on a slip of paper and delivered it to his open book. He stopped.

2. Eventually say, "I'll take one more question" — not because you're spent, but because the audience has had enough.

3. Don't complain about anything from the podium. Anything! You had to get up at 5 A.M. to get here? Boo-hoo. There are MFA students and unpublished writers listening who'd be only too willing and grateful to set their alarms for any hour, without bellyaching. You complain that writing is such hard work and so lonely? You brat: try digging ditches or disabling IEDs or doing a thousand other harder things for a living.

4. Buy some books yourself, especially those by today's unfamous and ignored. Tomorrow they'll win prizes.

COUPLING COLUMNS

Boy Meets Girl

I ONCE FROWNED THROUGH an episode of *The Oprah Winfrey Show* featuring marriageable Alaskan males in search of wives. Every flannel-clad guy was hoping for a gal who shared his passions, i.e., fishing, hunting, and snowmobiling. Oprah did not challenge the basic thesis — that eligibles who dogsled together, bed together — nor did she ask, "Why all this comradeship? Why not hunt and fish among yourselves and meet the ladies for dinner?"

I am not against hobbies, just the elevation of them to a relationship prerequisite. My bias springs from my own lack of intergender interests and my conviction that togetherness is overrated. My parents were happily married for forty-five years. Did my mother ever toss a football around with my father? Did he knit or sew or tend the tomatoes? He'd been a tennis player before he broke his ankles in the war; she never held a racket unless it was used to dislodge a cobweb from a light fixture.

Today's attenuated wedding announcements advance this modern theory, the one that says men and women find truest love on a raft or a lift line after the wasted years of dating sissies. Bridesmaids and siblings testify, too: how the featured bride and groom love the same obscure rock band, forage for the same mushrooms, ski telemark versus alpine, see only the films of Rainer Werner Fassbinder.

I do understand that putting forth one's common interests for the sake of matchmaking is more polite than asking for a certain size breast or bank account. But in private, in the office I would run if I were a professional matchmaker, I'd base my decisions on better predictors of compatibility than shared leisure pursuits. My questionnaire would ask: Do you have children? Do you want children? Are you religious or irreligious? How far ahead of your flight do you get to the airport? Are you willing to leave dirty dishes in the sink overnight? What percentage of the bill do you tip? How close to the screen do you sit at the movies? How often do you eat out/talk to Mom/pay bills? Can you fall asleep with the light on? Coffee or tea? Red state or blue?

This matchmaking impulse runs in my family, and our successes are an ode to randomness. My favorite stories celebrate love as accidents of luck and good timing. The best last-man-standing fix-up story belongs to my sister. Circa 1968, her then fiancé was driving from Cambridge to Amherst, Massachusetts, to visit her. "Could you find someone for Pete?" he asked before setting out. "We're leaving here at midnight." My sister canvassed Patterson Hall until she found a night-owl friend, Linda, the only girl awake at 2 A.M. Linda said okay, sure, I'll meet him. One year later: wedding bells.

Closely related to accidental love is the time-honored hunch. Good instincts help here, and a willingness to let the aphorism, "It's what's on the inside that counts," stand shoulder to shoulder with physical attraction. My friend Douglas indulged an excellent hunch when he was a bachelor of thirty-five. As a graduate student at Boston College he shared a big open office with five other teaching assistants, including Mary. One day her brother, a BC undergraduate, came by to visit and found her asleep at her desk. Douglas watched; he told me that he knew from the way Louis looked at his sleeping sister, with such fondness, that she had to be an extraordinarily good person. He asked Mary out that night and married her soon thereafter, almost forty years ago.

I was fixed up with my husband on the basis of not much more than our being in the social viewfinder of his cousin Jill. If we had hobbies to discuss on that first blind date, they didn't come up. Our joint extracurricular activities — aside from the son that trumps them all — have waxed and waned over the years. We lost interest in the running, the tennis, the cross-country skiing. He hasn't urged me to do anything I consider dangerous since I cried on the back of a Jet Ski in 1994. I prefer going solo to the driving range so I can hit in peace, without the unsolicited coaching. Every few years we stack the half cord of wood that a truck dumps on our driveway. And sometimes, when the right song comes on in our living room, we dance.

May I Recommend . . .

WE AGREED IN OUR YOUTH, easily and companionably, that we weren't going to have children. It was 1975 when we married, and our no-child avowal needed little defending in our circle. The one couple with a toddler seemed the odd pair out. "We had her during the baby bust," they liked to say, smiling in what I now recognize as insider knowledge, i.e., parental bliss. Bob and I did nothing rash — no tubes tied or vas deferens cauterized — but when we bought a house, our purchase and sale agreement stipulated that the backyard monkey bars would go with the seller.

In 1978, Bob's brother and his wife had Erica, our first baby relative. We spent vacations in California at her side, and photos of her — a miracle of recessive genes, her blond curls and blue eyes — appeared in every room of our house. Like grandparents, we had the best of all worlds: a baby to dote on whose shrieks of hunger were someone else's job to quell.

In 1980, one of my best friends had an unplanned baby girl. She was single and a lawyer working long hours, so none of it should have been easy. At thirty, I found myself visiting often after work, with a fascination masquerading as moral support. Motherhood began looking less tiresome and more enviable. During one visit, baby Julia was slumped sideways in her highchair, her mother laughing at nothing more than her adorableness, when I blurted out, "I've been thinking a lot about doing this." My friend turned sharply toward me, the baby spoon and cereal on its way to the little mouth, and she who was usually ironic and self-deprecating said solemnly, "It's the most wonderful thing in the world."

Not a week later, Bob and I were driving up Woodcliff Road toward Centre Street in Newton Highlands, Massachusetts, a moment and place frozen in memory, when he said quietly, "I've been thinking a lot lately about having a baby."

"Me too," I breathed.

And besides that simultaneous reproductive lightning bolt, here's where more luck came in: we didn't know if we had the physiological goods. We said, sitting on the edge of the bed, "Okay. We'll try. We'll give it a year. If it doesn't happen, we won't go crazy." Cyclically speaking, the first opportunity came in two weeks, so we did what was medically required, then did it again the next night for good measure. I took my temperature as a follow-up, which might have told the tale if I'd known what I was looking for. Two weeks passed, then a significant third. I was late. This was before the days of home pregnancy tests, which now seems prehistoric — a visit to a lab, a blood test, the wait. At the appointed hour, I dialed the doctor's number and stated my name. The nurse paused, then, in a buoyant singsong I remember to this day, whispered, "Congratulations."

A few hours officially pregnant, we made phone calls: to our parents, to siblings, to Aunt Hattie in West Palm Beach. My father reportedly slid to the floor in ecstasy. That phone bill, with the pertinent calls of May 20, 1981, circled in felt-tip pen, is the opening souvenir in what became Benjamin's first photo album. Below it: me in a pink sundress, not showing but grinning, and the Polaroid of my first ultrasound.

I'll stop there, because every parent has a birth story and everybody loves their children. Until now, I haven't proselytized in print out of respect for those who can't and those who don't want Pollyanna promoting parenthood. But yesterday was Ben's birthday, and because I'm convinced he's the best idea we ever had, such sentiments move a mother to write about what she might have missed.

What if we'd been the husband and wife in my cautionary tale, a true one, about a childless couple who stuck to their guns? They spearheaded a support group called Nonparents Anonymous and were quoted in the *Boston Globe* decades ago describing the freedom, the spontaneity, the money saved, the creativity nurtured, blah blah blah. Today I know through mutual friends that they are divorced. But not just divorced;

divorced and furious. The ex-wife claims he ruined her life with his nonparent nonsense. He says it's her own damn fault. She left town, postmenopausal, never to be heard from again. He's single, eligible, and searching for a wife of childbearing age.

I Want to Know

I'VE LONG BEEN GRATEFUL to the nice woman who left the buffet table at a West Springfield, Massachusetts, restaurant to alert me to the mortifying fact that my skirt was tucked into the waistband of my pantyhose as I exited the ladies' room.

Doesn't everyone appreciate this brand of human mirrordom? Don't we all want a friend or partner who, in public, can pantomime *lipstick on teeth* or *fly unzipped*? I remember with great fondness the boss who asked me with a wry smile, "New dress?" the day I came to work with a price tag still hanging from my armpit.

My enthusiasm for grooming frankness leads me to overfascination with couples who exercise none. Most memorably: a happy pair, or so it seemed, one child of each gender at home, who sat next to me at a dinner party, circa 1990.

I don't recall the food or the guest list, only the undisturbed nor'easter of dandruff resting on the husband's collar, evidently unnoticed, unbrushed, unscolded by his wife all night.

I asked two professionals about this. Was it delicacy? Embarrassment? Cluelessness? How does one account for toupees? The first explained, "It could be habituation. You get used to something and don't see it anymore. Also, there are dynamics within couples. If you're together, and you tell someone, for example, that his T-shirt is ripped and he smells, and he gets mad, you don't tell him anymore. It's probably the iceberg dynamic: You the outsider are seeing a moment, and you ask yourself, 'How could she let him come to dinner like that?' But you may be seeing the tip of a twenty-year struggle. She's reached the point where she says, 'If he wants to embarrass himself, it's not my problem.'"

The other professional I consulted didn't get psychoanalytic. He launched into a diatribe about a clueless wife in his social circle. "She's dressed to kill! All she cares about is her own appearance. And even though husband wears five-thousand-dollar custom-made suits, the hair growing out of his nose is so thick that I wonder how he can breathe. Why doesn't she say something?"

I brought up the subject of my mother, a dainty and impeccable woman, happily married to my father, a slob. They'd arrive at my house and I'd say, "Dad? Your tie. It's covered with spots." My mother would whirl around and snap — she who'd

just driven two hours in the company of that soiled outfit —
"Lou! Your tie! What's wrong with you?"

Nothing, I'm sure. In retrospect I view my father's stains
as evidence of his good character. He wore them with pride,
judging fastidious men to be vain peacocks and phonies. And
my mother: When she looked in the mirror, she concentrated
on the immediate self. Habituation didn't refract or reflect
my father in the background, holes in his sweaters, eyeglasses
askew.

Just as often, it's the man who embodies *Love is blind*. I will
see a woman — around sixty, miniskirted, wearing plastic earrings wired with colored lights, her hair high and black, better suited to a flamenco troupe — and next to her the button-
down husband in gray pinstripes, looking unmindful of the
spectacle that is his wife.

A friend helped explain this phenomenon. She said her husband of forty-plus years doesn't notice anything. "If I gained
a hundred pounds, he wouldn't notice. If I've had a drastic
haircut and I ask, 'Notice anything new?' I see a look of panic
on his face. 'New dress?' he might say. Since that time, he au-
tomatically answers, 'Got your hair cut?' I don't know if he's
locked into some version of me from long ago, something
ideal that never was. It's really annoying."

Perhaps I live in an overly frank family. My husband has
an expression that I call "evaluative." His features rearrange
themselves into something that is part squint, part frown, a
look I've seen on the faces of judges at the Westminster Dog

Show. Occasionally he undergoes a moment of delicacy before blurting out what the offense is, but most often he diagnoses and prescribes without much soul-searching. My son will say, "Ma? You're not planning to wear those pants outside the house, are you?"

Not now, I won't.

A Mister and Missus

Michael Rustigan, a California criminologist, said he wonders how Rader, if he is the BTK killer, could hide a sinister life from his wife. "You can fake 'nice guy' at work," he said. "But how do you fake 'nice guy' when you're married?"

— ASSOCIATED PRESS

AT FIRST I WAS PUZZLED by the purported wedded bliss of Mr. and Mrs. Dennis Rader of Park City, Kansas. Mr. Rader has been charged with ten murders and has confessed to six, leading onlookers to conclude that Mr. Compartmentalize had found his perfect mate in Ms. Clueless. Not that I'm toasting any newlyweds with references to that paradigm, but still I think their marital success lies in the widely quoted forensic fact that this husband "had gone 27 years without communication."

I wish Paula Rader and her two adult children well, but I'll still need to watch Diane Sawyer ask the excruciating questions in prime time: *Nothing? No hint? No unexplained absences, no penchant for long walks, no suspicious midnight loads of laundry? No funny stuff with knots?*

"Not really," Mrs. Rader might say, tissue wadded in her fist, wedding portrait at her elbow.

Is it possible that Mr. Rader didn't raise her suspicions? I think so. I remember reading about a man who worked for the CIA for decades whose family thought he was a higher-up with the U.S. Postal Service. Novelist Anita Shreve has said that after she wrote *The Pilot's Wife,* the story of a man with two wives and two families, she received hundreds of letters from people asking, "How is this possible? Who could keep such secrets?" at the same time dozens wrote to say, "You told my story. This is what happened to me."

I will not grade Mrs. Rader on her lack of inquisitiveness or shabby powers of observation. At dinner I ask my husband of twenty-nine years what happened at work that day and he says, "Nothing." I rarely press him. He means, "I don't particularly want to report on the ins and outs of today's frustrations, which would be just like yesterday's." We move on to other topics, other people, especially our son. He likes to hear about my work, my phone calls from what he considers interesting places — editors, agents, friends. I'm not a shrink. I don't interrogate him because I like to have my thoughts to myself sometimes. How annoying would it be to live with someone who asked constantly what I was thinking and feeling: *What does that faraway look on your face mean? Happy? Sad? In between?*

A friend of mine recently turned up with a new beau of the highly sensitive variety. He inquired in therapeutic fashion upon first meeting me: *Who are you? What do you worry about?* It reminded me of a job interview endured by a friend at which the prospective employer asked earnestly, "How would you describe the Who of you and the What of you?" Her first stab at a gossamer answer was rejected as being only the What of her.

I have discovered that the old bromide, "Never go to bed angry" (translation: discuss and make up), is not for everyone. One of my husband's most endearing qualities is that he wakes up in a good mood, the slate clean. If there's been what a friend's polite parents call a "mister and missus," i.e., a little spat, it tends to fade rather than fester overnight. I suppose some of you will say, "That's what *you* think. Discuss it. Communicate. Fix it."

But it's only a "mister and missus." Not unrelated, CNN reported last year that men simply have fewer feelings than women. That was enlightening news and applicable science. Why make husbands discuss and analyze and debrief feelings they aren't endowed with? Besides, the unexamined life has much to recommend it, couple-wise. In my case, 29 years times 365 days would have meant a lot of tedious pulse-takings and conversational detritus. Which brings me back to the Raders, married thirty-four years. If she had asked, "Where were you tonight?" he would have said, "At church with my fellow deacons. At Cub Scouts, hon. Tying knots." Maybe follow-up questions annoyed him, made him leave the table. Or worse. Maybe Mrs. Dennis Rader found there was a fine line between parallel lives and harmony.

Monsieur Clean

MY SISTER-IN-LAW'S sister-in-law, a mother of three, once told me that when she's bored, she cleans. I admire that impulse the way I might admire perfect pitch or fluency in a foreign language, which is to say outside myself and constitutionally unattainable in this incarnation.

It used to be that my husband and I had the same threshold for neatness — elastic — but something has shifted. Since he turned fifty, he hates clutter, sees it everywhere, including what I consider to be well-groomed piles of saved mail, notes to self, and unread magazines. In psychoanalyzing this midlife fastidiousness, I blame two things: Our son left for college in the fall of 2000, narrowing the population of non–neat freaks in the home to one: me. And second, my husband's family of origin.

They are immaculate, none more than his paternal grandmother, who lived with Bob growing up, who would fold the contents of everyone's drawers, who wrapped her own underwear in tissue paper, who scrubbed the inside of the dishwasher, who moved every year to a new (as in newly built/never sullied) apartment. Within my family, we were neat, but we weren't frantic. The living room smelled like lemon oil, and that seemed like plenty. We admonished those more compulsive than ourselves, "Don't be Cousin Sophie," a tribute to the relative famous for clearing the table while others were still eating.

Bob's meticulousness ratcheted up a notch in 2003 after *Publishers Weekly* ran an interview with me. Before the reporter came to the house, I hid the junk, vacuumed, made coffee, even made the beds. When the interview ran, it described me in my "cheerfully cluttered kitchen," which I found adorable. Bob did not. Suddenly countertop essentials — vases filled with wooden utensils, pepper mills, the bagel guillotine, the ibuprofen, a cutting board or two, the spoon rests — looked ominously to him like the un-put-away.

Are you asking, "If he cares so much, why doesn't *he* clean up?" Well, he does. Weekend mornings he's at his tidiest and therefore most annoying. When I'm in a good mood, I find the hum of the carpet sweeper, a tic while he's watching TV, mildly amusing. But other days, the whir of that mechanical brush lapping up the sunroom's crumbs sounds like a rebuke. He looks up and sees me frowning. "I'm cleaning," he says. "What's wrong with that?"

"It's your body language," I grumble. "I know you: You're

saying, 'I work all week and I shouldn't have to be cleaning up after you.'" I have resorted to name-calling: Mr. Clean. Hazel. Sue Ann Nivens.

I am neat in ways that don't count on the Bob scale: I disinfect my sponges regularly in the microwave or dishwasher. I maintain an accordion file of clipped recipes that are divided into categories and graded. My spices are alphabetized, and my closet is arranged by color. I have my strengths, just as Bob has his weaknesses. I accuse him of being, in the words of Holden Caulfield, a secret slob, the out-of-sight-out-of-mind kind of housekeeper. Whereas I can put my hands on an RSVP card as its deadline approaches and never pass through a stationery department without augmenting my supply of file folders, he shoves everything into drawers. I recycle. He keeps radiology journals that date back to Madame Curie.

If it were sexism, I'd complain louder, but it's DNA: Grandma Hinka's values visited, late in life, upon the grandson. He'd want any roommate, wife or no wife, to be crazy clean. I do try, because I understand that immaculate quarters are more gratifying than a pigsty. He is capable on some nights of hiding his dismay at the mess that I call cooking because dinner is on the table and cumin's in the air.

We'll work it out. I have called for a morning grace period: Allow me to eat my toast before I must refrigerate the butter and wash the cup I'm drinking from. I appeal to his scientific side: One shouldn't swab the decks with the bacteria-laden sponge at the same time one is prepping food, should one?

I've heard that some women grab a comb and lipstick when their husband pulls into the driveway. *What's so difficult?* I ask myself. *After all these years, don't I know how to put a smile on his face?* The back door opens. I shove the potato peels down the disposal, and, with rubber-gloved hands, I wave.

Ego Boundaries

MY HUSBAND HAS excellent taste, inherited from his late father, a sharp dresser with an impeccable eye, whose favorite cultural institution when visiting Boston was Filene's Basement. Though not a slave to fashion, my husband likes his wife to dress in what he views as elegant yet tasteful attire. And the best way to achieve this, he once believed, was to accompany me on shopping trips.

In my less confident youth, I complied. I even solicited his vote on a dress that was my first choice for a rather special occasion — our wedding. He didn't like it. I still remember it longingly: two-piece, a bit Edwardian, ivory silk crepe yet affordable. "Are you sure?" I asked, as if a fiancé belonged in a bride's dressing room. He was sure. I retreated.

Might you have expected more fashion backbone from a woman who graduated from college the year *Ms.* magazine was launched? Yes. I didn't have then what I've developed over many decades of marriage: the ability to overrule him and find a cure for, at least in this context, that wifely condition, the disease to please.

Our son helped. Somewhere in his teenage years, after his dad criticized something or other — haircut, sneakers, item of clothing — Ben said, "Ego boundaries, Dad." It seemed so simple and good-natured, yet so profound. I can't report that my husband's feedback mechanism is so finely tuned that he answered with, "You're right. You are not me and vice versa." We still have to invoke this phrase on a regular basis to remind Mr. Arbiter of Taste that my ruffled chili-red scarf from the local arts festival is wrapped around my neck and not his. I hasten to add that I don't have oddball taste in clothes. I am not one of those women who calls attention to herself by sewing sequins on her bodices or gluing feathers to her eyeglasses. My taste, I insist, is separate but equal, just a touch more . . . idiosyncratic.

What I've learned over the years is that I can wear him down, sartorially speaking, as if administering a series of allergy shots. I expose him to the offensive element — say, a tweed swing jacket, circa 1940, that I paid $50 for. "The white gloves," he notes, gazing forlornly at the complete ensemble. "Now it's a costume." I remove the gloves for another day, for dinners with friends who will leave their husbands and loden coats at home. Compromise, I've heard, is helpful within the institution of marriage.

My late-in-life confidence was born of practicality: I was

leaving to catch a plane, heading for the West Coast, donning swing jacket number two, pale yellow wool, mint condition. "Please," Bob begged again. "Please don't." Did I mention that this was a solo trip? That he was fretting about what I'd be seen in three thousand miles away? Not only did I leave wearing the hated coat, but I was able to report from Seattle and San Francisco, "Thank goodness I overruled you. It's blustery out here."

I'd estimate that ninety percent of the time, I wear what I want to wear. One still needs those mutually agreed upon outfits for events like the office holiday party, his camp, where ego boundaries are a little fuzzier. And, okay, I still don't wear in his presence the darling nylon blouses, circa 1950, or the beaded sweater he doesn't realize is very much back in style. That's me being peaceable. I have plenty of other options, so why make him squirm? Again, marital longevity loves compromise.

My most recent victory involved a silk flower pin, an orange tiger lily. How great it looked on my black turtleneck, and how perfect to wear to lunch at my mother-in-law's retirement village. "Not that," Mr. Arbiter begged. "I hate it." I smiled and explained: Ladies of a certain age would love it. It was both old and new, a little Edna St. Vincent Millay and a little *Sex and the City*. He didn't care. He hated that show. I didn't budge. When I entered the dining hall, first Rita gasped, then Thelma, then Sylvia, then Essie, in admiration of my boutonniere. Essie herself was sporting a fabric red rose. She told me that I should go to the millinery district in New York, where I could buy many such adornments for a song.

Bob smiled the smile of the vanquished. "He loves to come shopping with me," I explained.

I Married a Gourmet

WHEN I MET BOB, he was twenty-two and renting a basement apartment under a funeral home in Boston's Kenmore Square. His meal plan was boyish and homely: steak, stewed tomatoes, creamed corn, and frozen bagels. He told me he didn't like chicken or fish, which put two check marks in the minus column, boyfriend-wise. A taste for fish was important in my family; my maternal grandparents had immigrated from Riga, Latvia, and my grandmother was famous for the depth and breadth of her haddock repertoire.

It wasn't long before I realized that Bob *did* like fish and poultry, but that his mother had baked hers until the internal temperature no longer registered on a thermometer. His taste buds had been desiccated and led astray; they needed a guide, a helpmeet, a girl who had the Baltic in her DNA.

Because he was in graduate school and I earned $8,500 a year, our restaurant dates meant hot turkey sandwiches,

Dutch, at the Linwood Bar and Grill ($2). Occasionally we'd splurge and order the roast turkey dinner ($3). Recognizing us as regulars, a kind waitress slipped us saucers of extra meat with a wink. Shrimp in lobster sauce on Queensberry Street seemed haute enough, as did advancing from pepperoni to anchovy pizzas. Bob started paying attention to wine, and I stopped putting ice cubes in my Chianti.

Food got fashionable around the time our jobs paid more. We bought our first Cuisinart in 1977; a wok in '79, a fish poacher in '80, a coffee grinder in '85. Things escalated: pasta went fresh, rice became basmati, mushrooms were dried, fish was raw. Bob discovered the Food Channel and many things his wife was doing wrong. Did I skin my tomatoes before making a sauce? Were my bay leaves from Turkey or California?

This is how far we've traveled, gastronomically: I am known to murmur over dinner, after Bob confides that my osso buco isn't quite as good as last time, "It's tough living with a restaurant critic." I grouse a little. I tell him it took three hours, and maybe he'd like to send it back. Maybe he'd prefer a nice can of Progresso after a hard day's work.

"Do you want me to lie and say I love it?" he asks. He points out that which is true, and what makes me pay attention to the feedback: When he likes something, he's rapturous. If our company holds back, Bob doesn't wait for guests to say, "This is delicious." He speaks right up. Last time we had company, I made roasted pears. The guests were having an animated discussion that wasn't about dessert. Bob dug in. I heard a moan, a private ecstatic whimper. Then another.

"Good?" I asked.

"This," Bob said with great conviction, as if he hadn't said it a hundred times before, "is the best thing I ever ate."

Food appreciation of this magnitude leads to cooking, which leads to his kitchen rituals: First, he consults eight or nine favorite cookbooks and searches them for virgin territory. He calls out his nominees: The cassoulet! The black cod with the red-miso glaze! To which I say, "Do we have to? The salmon on the grill with the mesquite is so nice." Step two: indefatigable shopping. If the recipe calls for black mustard seeds and mine are brown, he volunteers to jump in the car and drive to . . . Where might he find black mustard seeds, or mache instead of frisée, or lamb from New Zealand rather than Northampton? I explain: chefs expect owners of their cookbooks to be flexible. Toasted pignoli suggested for a garnish? Sorry; I thought I had some. No one will miss them. Sometimes I have to lie for his peace of mind. I don't tell him that I padded the *polpette* with a little ground chicken because I didn't have enough ground veal. Step three: assembly. *Mise en place.* Consult wife as to whereabouts of measuring spoons, measuring cups, garlic, lemon, grater, colander, and tahini.

Step four: sharpen the knife, this way and that, steel against steel, like an infomercial host, a fencer on KP. "What?" he asks me, frowning in the doorway. "Am I *not* supposed to sharpen the knife?"

I retreat at this point, before he asks me what country the olive oil is from.

"Bob made it," I tell the company when they compliment the soup.

The chef takes a sip and frowns. "Not as good as last time," he says.

I Sleep Around

I AM SOMETHING OF an expert in matters of annoying a husband when he's trying to sleep. There's the ritual of the emollients, involving hand cream, moisturizer, and lip gloss. There's the thermostat, set too high, requiring discussion and/or adjustment. There's my forgotten vitamin pill, two floors away in the kitchen. Or the porch light still burning, the e-mail unreturned, the water glass unrefreshed, the afghan off-kilter, the cable box on. In other words, this is about a twitchy wife and her marital bed, by which I mean the site of sleep, and not that other, more commonly and sensationally referenced thing: sex.

"Please sleep downstairs," my husband groans, after imploring me to shut off the light and reminding me of his breadwinning 6 A.M. alarm.

He is not unreasonable. He gets up at dawn, works very hard, and is exhausted most nights. Pillow talk is largely one-sided: I arrange myself, tuck the covers under my arms, flounce around while I choose whether to face east or west. Only seconds have passed when I say, "Good night, hon," to which he moans, "Huh? Whah? You woke me up." Despite this talent for nearly narcoleptic nodding off, he requires total blackout conditions in order to fall asleep, which correlate negatively with my need to read. I argue halfheartedly and insincerely, one foot off the mattress, book and glasses in hand, "If you can nap in the middle of the day with the TV on, why is total darkness and silence essential? Isn't that hypocritical?"

"I have to get up at six," I hear again.

Why argue? I love my holidays in the guest room. There I find nothingness — no curfew, no rules and regs, no remote control. "Of course," I cluck on my way out. "You get up so early. And you have such a hard day tomorrow. I'll go downstairs. I don't mind."

I've tried compromise. I've owned at least two of those miniature reading lights that hook onto your book and forestall marital spats, unless your bedfellow has transparent eyelids the way mine apparently does. Equally unsuccessful was an eye mask *pour l'homme,* the kind that Hollywood stars wore in movie-set boudoirs, but of the masculine variety: maroon silk patterned with golfers wearing knickers. He hated it. A mediator might say that flexibility is missing in our marriage around the subject of irreconcilable bedtimes. If only I *minded* losing to inflexibility; if only I was possessive of my half of the mattress or felt worried about it as a symbolic representation of sexual congress, I'd fight the good fight.

I shouldn't have made fun of President and Mrs. Nixon in the 1970s for, among other things, sleeping apart. I'm older and wiser now, and I've got a little insomnia myself. I'm sure that separate White House bedrooms were a metaphor for nothing conjugal. Was I too young and callow to allow that a thoughtful president who tosses and turns all night might bunk elsewhere for a first lady's sake?

Closer to home, neither one of us sees my furloughs as a romantic failure. It's a luxury to have an extra bedroom and a partner who doesn't miss you while he's down for the count. It's also about public health. At the first sign of a scratchy throat, his or mine, I volunteer to withdraw, to commence the quarantine. If it weren't politically incorrect — the assumption that all Americans had a spare bedroom — the Surgeon General would recommend, along with frequent hand washing, that sick spouses take their germs down the hall.

"Separate bedrooms" is an inaccurate and loaded phrase. Only royalty and the elderly can admit to it without drawing smirks. Accordingly, I am not recommending the formalization of any such thing. Your relatives would worry, your peers would gossip, and your spouse would look for outside gratification. When our son, now twenty-three, is visiting, I stay put lest he think there is something wrong with his parents' love life.

"What time did you come down to the guest room?" my

husband asks in the morning, always a little surprised, on his way to work. "Nine-ish," I say. "I wanted to read. I didn't want to keep you up."

Such wifely thoughtfulness induces a smile. I tell him he looks good because it's true. He slept well in that wide roomy bed, and it shows.

The Best Man

JULY 29, 2005, WAS OUR thirtieth wedding anniversary, a milestone I hesitate to announce due to the advanced age such marital longevity connotes. We did not throw a party or renew our vows; to do so would be out of character for a couple who barely threw a party the first time around. Our wedding was put together on short notice and was simplicity itself: four parents, one sister, her husband, who doubled as photographer, and eight friends. It took place on a Tuesday night in Brookline, Massachusetts. The rabbi officiating at Temple Ohabei Shalom had been a chaplain at UC Berkeley, which made him tolerant of a groom who requested "no religious mumbo jumbo."

Our formal engagement was pragmatism itself. Bob was starting an internship on July 1 and had won the booby prize in the vacation lottery: his would begin three weeks into the job. We had talked obliquely of marriage, without using that

noun and without a question being popped. Our understand-
ing, as my mother liked to call it, was that at the end of his
internship, that next June-ish, we'd . . . assemble the families.

Instead, in shotgun fashion, we made the necessary plans
— date, time, rabbi, restaurant. In a less-said-the-better mode,
we referred to the upcoming nuptials as "the party" and the
honeymoon as "the trip." I made my dress: off-white, knee-
length, one lily on my shoulder strap. Bob wore a new suit, a
new shirt, a new tie, which I kept for years. My parents sent
out announcements, resulting in both gifts and angry phone
calls from the uninvited. My mother explained rather grandly
that Bob, her new son-in-law — you see, he was a doctor, an
MD, an intern — had no time to plan a big wedding like my
sister's at La Sala de Puerto Rico, in the student center at MIT,
of which her other son-in-law, they might recall, was a graduate.

Our honeymoon was a gift from Bob's brother and sister-
in-law: a car trip around California, with them as guides, we
newlyweds in the back seat of their Vega, a Styrofoam food
chest between us, some nights in a three-man tent but most
at one Motel 6 or another, no reservations. But the Night to
Remember was an ammonia-scented cabin on Lake Tahoe
maintained by the Campus Crusade for Christ, which Mr. No
Religious Mumbo Jumbo dubbed the Church of the Immaculate Accommodations.

Admitting to a marriage of many decades brings a new
wrinkle. Strangers, upon hearing I have a grown son, often

ask if Ben is our child jointly, or just mine. "From a first marriage?" the rude person persists. It's not meant as a compliment, but I take it as one. They mean that hardly anyone they
know has been married long enough both to conceive a child
and attend his college graduation as an extant couple.

Can one talk about marital longevity without sounding
smug? I'll try. We don't preen about this. And if I'm sounding
overly of-the-people about Motel 6, let me confess that Bob
claims my idea of roughing it now is a hotel room without a
phone in the bathroom.

A few weeks ago, I pointed out to Bob that he had never
proposed to me. He surprised me by asking, "Want me to
propose now?" We were eating burgers at the Northampton
Brewery; i.e., this was no bended knee, no gondola in Venice.
It was 5:30 on a Wednesday night. "Nah," I said, "That's okay.
I'm sure the guys who popped the question on electronic
scoreboards are divorced by now."

I wouldn't dare theorize that cinematic romances and lav-
ish weddings are inversely proportional to long marriages. But
there are lots of us, the technically unproposed to, out there.
My friends Patty and Chuck, for example. She laughed out
loud when I asked how their marriage came about. "I was trying to get my first husband — we were separated — to buy me
snow tires for my Gremlin," she explained. "Chuck said, 'Get
rid of that guy, and I'll buy you snow tires.'"

"Wow," I said. "And that was it?"

"That was it," she confirmed. I thought back to their

twenty-fifth-anniversary party. Chuck toasted Patty and made excellent jokes at his own expense. She and I might have collaborated on a response, a renewed vow of sorts: Here's to the guys not on bended knee, not holding little velvet boxes. Here's to things more durable than diamonds.

SINCE THEN

This Is for You

FIVE YEARS AGO, when all was well, a *Boston Globe* editor asked if I'd like to be one of several regular contributors
to a proposed weekly column they planned to call Coupling.
I would fill, unofficially, the long-married slot, and my age
would appear in the italicized ID at the end of every piece
— good stuff revealed, please. Perhaps I'd like to write about
my grown son bringing women home?

"I'm not going to write about my son's love life," I said.
"And if I'm airing any dirty laundry of my own, I'd better ask
my husband."

When I ran it by Bob, he said, "Okay, as long as you don't
write about me."

Of course I wrote about nothing *but* him: Bob the over-
zealous foodie and restaurant critic at his own table. Bob the
dispenser of unsolicited advice on how to dress, clean house,
and swing a golf club. Bob the tired guy who was early to bed
and first to leave any party.

As a tribute to his good nature and husbandly pride, it took exactly two essays for him to enjoy his starring role, whether it was that of hero, villain, or punch line. Looking back at the columns I wrote, I see traits, fondly described and enlarged, of what was already creeping unrecognized into our lives: exaggerated behaviors. Neat and punctual Bob; Bob the noodge; Bob the proud husband and father who bragged too much. Between my own lines I see the earliest hints of his slipping into the brain disorder that would first change and diminish him, and then, three years and eight months later, kill him.

Friends ask if I'd write about this siege, and I always said no. Memoirs about losing a loved one are pretty much the same: he or she is well, then something's wrong, then it's worse, and a lucky life changes. So it's just going to be this, a final, unassigned Coupling column in honor of the husband who made "long married" a fresh and funny topic.

The cruel disease that felled him was frontotemporal dementia — rare, untreatable, and fatal — a disease that often turns its victims into violent and paranoid versions of their normal selves. Bob, however, just got more gregarious. Any form of inappropriateness in public consisted of his answering most greetings and questions such as "Two for dinner tonight?" with "My wife had a movie made." Once brilliant, dignified, elegant, and cool, he regressed, becoming sweeter, easier, more childlike, stubborn in new but benign ways. He was fifty-seven when my son and I recognized that something was amiss. His wit was gone. His conversation and responses were a loop of what neurologists call stereotypies — persistent repetition of acts and words. ("I quit my job . . . My brother died . . . I went to Dartmouth.")

Old habits (pacing, punctuality, prompt bill paying, neatness) became ritualistic and obsessive. Type A behavior became A plus. The former gourmet wanted only pizza, ice cream, spaghetti, macaroni and cheese, and frozen turkey dinners that harked back to his working mother's menu plan. No new restaurants, and the same dish ordered at the old familiar ones. If I cooked something from the old repertoire, once a favorite, he'd hover, worried and suspicious, unconvinced that he'd ever eaten this before or loved it.

On his fifty-ninth birthday, as we rode the subway to SoHo, I asked — in the way one would ask a child — "Isn't it wonderful that we can go to your favorite restaurant on your birthday?" to which he answered, "It's wonderful that we can go to my favorite restaurant on my birthday?" — the echolalia I'd been reading about but had failed to recognize until that moment.

Soon enough, he said only two things: "Do the stuff," which could mean close the blinds or call Ben or pay the bill or put both hands on the steering wheel in the proper driver-ed position. Eventually four words became his motto and answer to every question. "I'm a happy guy!" he'd assert, no matter the topic, the setting, the listener. "I'm a happy guy."

Still worse, nine months before he died, a doctor friend noticed the atrophying and twitching of muscles in Bob's hands and arms. It meant he had the worst complication of the illness, whereby ALS, Lou Gehrig's disease, appears in tandem.

Nine months passed in what now feels like a minute. His appetite diminished, his limbs shrank, and his weight dropped. A physical therapist, at her sixth and last visit, said kindly, "He's had enough. Let's not put him through this." His breathing became shallower and more labored. I called our doctor and then Hospice for the first time on a Friday afternoon in late September 2009. They came the next day, and the first visit turned out to be their last. Morphine was mentioned for the first time, but it was still for the weeks ahead. Did I need a volunteer? Someone could come on my birthday two weeks hence, so my son and I could go out . . . could celebrate. At 7:30 the next morning, I went upstairs to check on him. He was breathing irregularly and then he wasn't. "Bobby?" I whispered, in case he was merely asleep. I touched his chest, a weakling's poke. I put two fingers to his neck in search of his carotid pulse. There was something — a heart was beating. I ran for Ben, asleep downstairs. Back at Bob's side, I knew that the pulse I'd felt wasn't his at all, but mine.

That night a heartbroken Ben said, "I want to speak at the funeral." Within twenty-four hours I thought, *If he can do it, so can I.* We worked separately and independently down the hall from each other. We made no biographical or anecdotal assignments, yet the full and true Bob emerged, as if we had evenly divided the best and funniest between the two of us. *How could a son who'd been red-eyed for days write something that wouldn't break everyone's heart?* I worried. Yet he put everyone at ease, an opening laugh of recognition, with, "If this were a real and proper tribute to Dad, then this eulogy would have started about ten minutes ahead of schedule."

It was the best funeral ever, I like to say. There was a big crowd and a tightly controlled program — no ramblings from an open mike, no surprises. A pianist played standards, a soprano sang Mahler, three speakers and a rabbi. People laughed and cried, and in honor of Bob the Bullet, as he'd been nicknamed thirty years before by a golfing buddy, we were done in an hour.

Ben ended by saying, "It can be crushing to think what must have been going through his head during the final months, when the disease took its worst toll. But I take solace in the fact that he had a family who loved him more than anything . . . And that makes me a happy guy."

I went last, and I couldn't end without a tribute to the man, at twenty-seven, whom Bob would have called his greatest accomplishment. I said, "Benjamin in Hebrew means 'son of my right hand.' And if ever there was an exemplar and spokesperson for that name, it is he. For about a year, people were hinting if not insisting that I bring in help, but what they didn't understand was that *it* was hard, but Bob was easy. To borrow Thomas Friedman's description of his late mother: she put the *mensch* in dementia. And then when I still thought I could manage, the best help of all arrived: Ben announced, 'I'm coming home. It's going to get worse. I can't live with myself being so far away. And it's the right thing to do.'"

The night before Ben returned to Los Angeles, I poured

each of us a glass of wine, and we went into the living room for a task we'd been putting off. In front of the fireplace, we transferred Bob's ashes from the black plastic crematory box to a beautiful wooden one, of bird's-eye maple and bubinga. Engraved on the lid are the words, "Robert M. Austin, 1949–2009. Beloved by all."

We'd known from the beginning that there would be no sprinkling or parting with the only thing we had left. Ashes are sadder than I ever could have imagined. We told these far-removed remains that we missed him. We put the box back on the mantel and raised our glasses. I said, "Let's each tell a funny story about Dad." And so we did.

Watching the Masters by Myself

WHEN I WAS TWELVE, my parents bought a Cape across the street from Mount Pleasant Golf Club in Lowell, Massachusetts, a private nine-hole course with a low membership fee. My father took up the game with secondhand clubs toted in a golf bag from Goodwill. Even his golf balls were previously owned, fished from the course's brook by enterprising neighborhood kids. He played several times a week, late into the fall, weather permitting. Without a lesson, immune to the biomechanics of the game, unmoved by titanium and carbon graphite, he never improved.

I took up golf out of sheer proximity to the course and because members' children under sixteen could play for free. Before I ventured onto the first green, I studied an illustrated how-to book by Sam Snead. My father took me out on the course for the first time, chanting all the way to the first tee, "Keep your head down. Keep your head down." I did. I swung and made contact. With my eyes fixed on the ball, I didn't follow its flight. The thwack was just right. Forty-five-plus years later, I still remember the look on my father's face: not glee or pride, but amazement verging on scholarship dreams. The ball had flown a hundred yards. In my family, that was far.

My early promise did not earn me lessons, due to the family ennui about all things involving fees. I only dabbled, playing a half dozen holes after school a few times a week with an equally tepid player, my next-door neighbor, Patsy, whose live-in uncle was a perennial runner-up in the city golf championship. When I turned sixteen, the free play ended. A junior membership was not discussed.

In my midtwenties I married Bob, who'd played since childhood. My father treated him to nine holes at Mount Pleasant on spring and summer visits. Affection and a little bit of duty seasoned the pairing. "No one who's played as long as your dad," Bob marveled, "has ever had a worse swing."

Bob and I were a good pairing, leisure-time-wise: I liked the house to myself, and he liked nine holes a few times a month, thoughtfully scheduled so childcare wouldn't be all mine on a weekend. "Want to hit the white ball today?" he'd ask his various golfing buddies, always at the last minute, always scrambling for a tee time. With his long drives and low handicap, he galloped up the fairways, finishing in record time. "Back so soon?" I often murmured. "You know how other wives complain about being a golf widow?" he'd ask with a wry smile. "Mine says, 'Golf? Why don't you go to Scotland?'"

I took group lessons one spring at a local course because my newest novel had a minor golf theme. I was put most gratifyingly into the subdivision of women who weren't pathetic. Inspired, my friend Janet and I signed up for private lessons with the club pro. I bought myself clubs, golf shoes, a Nancy Lopez glove, balls with a pink-ribbon motif, and two golf shirts at a sportswear outlet in Manchester, Vermont. After a few weeks of lessons on weekday afternoons, we ventured out to play nine holes. I was terrible. We let every man play through. I didn't return for that kind of golf — the real thing, on a course, the game as actually played.

Still with something of an itch, I worked on my swing at the driving range. I hit the ball longer when Bob wasn't there. "This is what you're doing" — he'd demonstrate, club slicing, hips akimbo. Bob was not a man who believed that golf was for everyone. He wanted poetry in motion, the kind of thing he feared could not be coaxed from the daughter of Louie Lipman, perennial duffer.

How do two fans of a game — one who played well and the other not at all — find common ground and marital accommodation? We sat on the same couch, Bob biting his nails and me knitting, watching Tiger Woods.

Bob had little interest in the rest of the field, no feel for the underdog. If Tiger wasn't on the leader board by Saturday, Bob would give up, pull weeds, go to the driving range, leave the tournament watching to me. "Tiger just got a birdie," I'd yell. "Come back. He's within three. It'll be okay."

Bob died in September 2009, not unexpectedly — he had a rare and fatal brain disorder, frontotemporal dementia — but still too fast. When Tiger crashed his SUV into a tree two months later, I was expecting the worst. Something was missing from the reporting, I suspected. How could he survive if eyewitnesses saw him lying in the street? Would breaking news announce any minute that Tiger Woods — too talented for this earth — had lost his life? I thought, prematurely and melodramatically, *Thank goodness Bob doesn't have to see this.*

I was wrong. It wasn't fatal. It was a cut lip, a ticket for careless driving, and a fine of $164. Soon enough came the reports of his philandering, a gossipy topic I enjoy when the cheater is an officeholder or man of the cloth. I understood why everyone was talking about Tiger's moral lapses, but shouldn't they be talking neurology? Might he who is famous for brains without charm and robotic behavior be a little Aspergian?

Months passed, and then the announcement came: Tiger would play in the Masters. On the Monday before his much-anticipated return to competition, I set my iPhone alarm for 1:55 P.M. so I wouldn't forget his 2 P.M. press conference. All agree: He seemed human and was unscripted. When he smiled it was just to the right, remorseful degree.

A day later, commentators and pundits are annoying me with their criticism of the Nike commercial where Tiger's late father speaks to him. What's wrong with that — a dead person exerting a little influence over those left behind? I will eat dinner Sunday night in front of the television, like all the other tournaments when Tiger had the lead. I try not to anticipate the widow quotient in this upcoming weekend, but I know it will be high. An essay I wrote about Bob, his illness, decline, and death, appears in the *New York Times'* Modern Love column on this Masters Sunday. And while the camera pans the famous Augusta azaleas, I am watching the budding of thirty-four Barrett Browning daffodils — a gift that a friend planted a few weeks after Bob died, one for every year of our marriage.

Bob would have been so happy with Tiger on Thursday, his lowest score ever at Augusta on day one. By Friday he is still high on the leader board, and after fifty-four holes on Saturday he is within reach. An announcer reminds me at the end of Phil Mickelson's third round that both his mother and wife are being treated for cancer. By Sunday I'm beginning to feel that kind and faithful Phil is my man this year. Still, I am nervous whenever Tiger addresses the ball. He is Bob's man. His bogeys kill me.

Bob isn't present in any otherworldly way, but old habits fade slowly. I yell as if he's just out in the yard, "A hole in one!" And then correct myself, the worst announcer and color commentator golf ever had — "No, sorry — it was an eagle." Eyes lowered onto my knitting, I had missed his first shot.

Phil is everyone's sentimental favorite, a lefty, the nice guy with three children, the embodiment of family values. Already in the lead, he birdies the eighteenth and wins. He hugs his faithful caddy and then strides, purposefully, devotedly, into the arms of his wife. I haven't forgotten that she almost died in childbirth, and an interventional radiologist saved her life. I'm a big fan of radiologists. Bob was one. They hug for twenty-seven seconds, and then they kiss. The camera zooms in. Tears are streaming down his sunburned face. No eye tuned to CBS is dry.

How would a post-scandal, post-hiatus Tiger win have looked? In my own version, I had dared to picture dishonored Elin surprising him, one beautiful child in each arm, at the edge of the eighteenth green, inspiring a sob of old like that between Tiger and Mr. Woods.

E-mails come in every few minutes about my essay in the *Times*. The condolence daffodils are near full bloom outside the window where I watch TV. Some readers write and tell me Bob must be smiling down at the loving portrait I've written. Smiling down? Even if I believed in that sort of thing, it would not be true today. Tiger has come in fourth.

We ♥ New York

IT MIGHT HAVE BEEN our Merrimack Valley connection — I was born in Lowell, Massachusetts, and he in neighboring Lawrence — or simple pride for Jews on TV (Sandy Koufax, Michael Landon, Steve Allen, Groucho Marx, Gertrude Berg). But mostly the draw was how Leonard Bernstein spoke directly to me at home, live from Carnegie Hall. In a family that had no hi-fi, no stereo, just an FM radio and classical leanings, I was put before our black-and-white TV to watch Bernstein's *Young People's Concerts with the New York Philharmonic,* which CBS began broadcasting in 1958. Most memorable moment? A child in the audience (Imagine living in New York! Imagine sitting so close to the stage!) asks Bernstein how Beethoven could have composed such beautiful music if he was deaf. "Think about how *Twinkle, Twinkle, Little Star* sounds," our teacher said, then turned around and played its first seven notes. Unlike me, he could play by ear without looking at the keys. "You can hear it in your head, can't you?" he asked us. "Well, Beethoven could hear the notes in his head, too."

What other lesson from a television show do I remember almost fifty years later? None. And what was my attention based on? Not professional dreams. (When my piano teacher had what used to be called a nervous breakdown, she winnowed her students down to a list that didn't include me.) Not Bernstein's wild exuberance on the podium, because my father, whose opinions I was prone to adopt, found Bernstein too theatrical. My loyalty was something closer to a biographical infatuation that a little Jewish girl might have for a celebrated Massachusetts man with humble roots, who played his first notes on a secondhand upright piano.

Decades later I let Tom Wolfe's brilliant, scathing, and hilarious book of essays, *Radical Chic and Mau-Mauing the Flak Catchers,* tarnish Mr. Bernstein in my affections. "Radical Chic" describes a cocktail party at the Bernsteins' thirteen-room duplex apartment on Park Avenue, its goal to introduce the Beautiful People to the Black Panther Party and perhaps aid their cause. Wolfe quotes Black Panther speaker Donald Cox lecturing, "Our Minister of Defense, Huey P. Newton, has said if we can't find a meaningful life . . . maybe we can have a meaningful death . . . and one reason the power structure fears the Black Panthers is that they know the Black Panthers are ready to die for what they believe in, and a lot of us have already died."

Wolfe continues, describing the scene. "Lenny seems like a changed man. He looks up at Cox and says, 'When you walk into this house, into this building' — and he gestures vaguely as if to take it all in, the moldings, the sconces, the Roquefort morsels rolled in crushed nuts, the servants, the elevator attendant and the doormen downstairs in their white dickeys, the marble lobby, the brass struts on the marquee out front — 'when you walk into this house, you must feel infuriated!'

"Cox looks embarrassed. 'No, man . . . I manage to overcome that . . . That's a personal thing . . .'

"'Well,' says Lenny, 'it makes *me* mad!'"

Uh-oh. Did I let his noblesse oblige color my portrait of the great man? I'm afraid I did during the judgmental 1970s. Now I say, so what? The record shows energy, generosity, genius, and selflessness. A normal Bernstein Saturday, as reproduced on his handwritten calendar page for December 1, 1956, reads, "11 A.M. Young People's Concert at Carnegie. 8 P.M. 'Candide' opening."

I live across the street from Carnegie Hall now, in the very apartment building where Bernstein wrote *West Side Story*. For months the opening bars of "Somewhere (There's a Place for Us)" — background music for an oft-running TIAA-CREF commercial — brought tears to my eyes. *I always knew you'd end up here,* this anthem said.

A Fine Nomance

WHEN I STARTED WRITING my tenth novel, *The View from Penthouse B,* it was going to be about four unrelated strangers living under one roof, a tale told in the third person by a young woman I couldn't quite get a grip on. After my husband's death, after not writing for six months, I reconfigured the story. Soon it was about middle-aged sister roommates; its first-person narrator, Gwen-Laura Schmidt, had been widowed eighteen whole months longer than I, and her late husband had died suddenly, nonautobiographically, from an undiagnosed malformation of a heart valve.

Gwen, though lovable, was stagnating socially. She hadn't started dating nor did she want to. She barely left the apartment. Unemployed as well, Gwen had a bad moneymaking idea — to create a mild-mannered escort service for people seeking nothing more than a platonic dinner and a peck on the cheek. As she says herself as early as page 2, "So far, it's only a concept, one that grew out of my own social perspective . . .

The working title for my organization is 'Chaste Dates.' So far, no one finds it either catchy or appealing."

Meanwhile, in my nonfictional life, the months passed. Unlike Gwen, I didn't mope around. My son told me it was time to travel, so I did. I applied and received a fellowship for one month's residency in Italy. I went to Mexico to teach a workshop and to Aspen for another. Soon enough, a year had passed, the span of time in all cultures that signals to your friends that you should at the very least consider dating.

I told them I was not interested. Had no inclination. When pressed I said, "Maybe, if that day comes, I'd be okay with a high school romance."

When asked what that meant, I said, "You know: someone likes you and you like him back. You go out on dates. Dinners in a well-lit restaurant. Maybe you'll kiss."

"Sex?" they often asked, not the least bit tentatively.

"High school romance," I repeated, which in my late-blooming case meant no.

Meanwhile, back in Penthouse B, my narrator wasn't moving forward socially either, which meant the plot was in danger of what in fiction workshops we call stasis. I knew what I had to do: send her out on a date and eventually get her laid, despite her disinclination.

She had two counselors in this matter: her sister and the other boarder in Penthouse B, Anthony, age twenty-nine, gay and helpful. I launched her with a tiptoe into classified waters. Under pressure from her roommates, she would write a personal ad. Finally, she composed one to run in the dignified

New York Review of Books. The headline in boldface was **Nervous.** Below that: "I was widowed 2+ years ago & have been sitting on the sidelines of my own life. This ad has less 2 do w/ me wanting 2 find love & more 2 do w/ pushing myself out the door. Looking for kind M 40–60 with similar ambivalences."

At the same time, in real life, one year and five months into widowhood, I told a very close friend that I might accept her invitation to meet the man she'd once mentioned, the nice one she'd served on a committee with/had spoken so highly of.

Thus I told people I was going on my first date since the Nixon administration. I Googled the fellow. The good news was interesting job and "Yale graduate." The bad news: he'd been a member of the class that made him seventy-five years old. I called my matchmaking friend and said a little indignantly, "He's seventy-five!"

"Is he?" she asked airily. "I don't notice those things," adding, "He's adorable. Think of it as a training date."

I did go to dinner with the man, who *was* extremely nice, interesting, smart, a good conversationalist — and he laughed at my jokes. I said yes to a second date and then a third, reasoning that if I turned him down merely because I had no interest in being his lady friend, what did that say about my character?

When the request came via e-mail for a fourth date, I worked hard to compose a turndown that would signal *no mas* rather than *rain check*. After much revision, I wrote back that I was "busy for the next few weeks" (true) and also "experiencing off-season hibernation inclinations." The very well-brought-up gentleman grasped what I was saying and wrote back politely if not elegantly.

Later that week, as phony retroactive research for my character, I went to the personals section of the *New York Review of Books*. One ad caught my eye: a male; the age was in the right range; a professional, a man of intellectual interests and high accomplishment. Should I write to that box number? Dare I? But there were overlapping bio snippets with the previous fellow — his profession, his "Southern gentleman," his "Hamptons," his cultivation of heirloom tomatoes. I called the friend who fixed me up and read the ad to her. "Don't answer! It's him!" she cried. "He cut a decade off his age, but they all do that."

What are the odds, I asked, that the first time in my life I nearly respond to a personal ad, its author is the one man I training-dated? It was all I needed to retreat from social outreach of the coed variety.

The novel expanded, but Gwen's social circle did not. It was May 2011. I sent my narrator to a fictional seminar called "Fine, I'll Go Online."

What's a verisimilitude-conscious author to do but join herself? I did. I also joined JDate and OkCupid, figuring *in for a penny, in for a pound*. A few responses trickled in. The highlights (meaning anecdotal as opposed to romantic):

There was the man, fresh from a yearly checkup with his internist, who announced over lunch that his doctor told him he didn't drink enough water.

"How does *he* know?" I asked.

After only a slight pause he said, "Because my stool is hard."

There was one who stuck his Nicorette gum under the chair . . . another who laughed at every single thing he or I uttered and who texted his girlfriend in New Jersey while sitting next to me at *The Help* . . . the man who asked me nothing about *my* life but went into so much detail about his that I came away knowing that his daughter was transferring from one college to another because the current school required its cheerleaders to perform backflips, whereas the future institution did not.

There was the astrologically inclined one whose second wife had the same birthday as I. And there was the actor who'd been the sixth husband of one of the stars of *The Golden Girls*.

Soon afterward, I quit every service before my membership expired. Then with my index finger literally on Match .com's Remove button, I remembered that I was mining some sentences for fictional use. (For example: "I wish to meet a woman as engaged in their own project: writing, performing, Visual Artist or yet to be classified — but not a Mime, as I am.")

For the first time in weeks, I looked at that morning's daily matches. There was one fellow who caught my eye: he looked smart and nice and normal. I clicked on him and reached his profile page. There I read about his marital status (divorced) and then his answers to the boilerplate questions about education, profession, pets, exercise, favorite places, favorite entertainment, and so forth down the list to last book read. His answer: "Elinor Lipman's *The Family Man.*"

I was stunned. Do I write back and reveal myself as a woman accomplished enough to publish novels yet trolling for dates on Match.com? After a few minutes, I clicked on "Send him an e-mail" and wrote, "That was lovely to see. Thank you. Elinor L."

He answered that night. He wrote very well, explaining how he'd become a fan of my books. He had an interesting job and a master's degree. He knew how to use a semicolon. After another exchange of e-mails, we made a plan, which turned into a three-hour dinner. A great date, in my opinion.

Here is where you mustn't get your hopes up. At this writing, eleven months have passed and we are what I can only call friends. Of course behind his back I call him "my insignificant other," my "friend without benefits," and "my imaginary boyfriend." I refer to what we have as "a nomance." He is excellent company, and our outings are, while not romantic, datelike, in that we are two straight people of different genders who often share an appetizer and have lively conversations.

But the following is what happens when you have close girlfriends who want to be bridesmaids at your future wedding: They hate your nonboyfriend, despite never having met him.

They think he should be (their words) thanking his lucky stars and/or madly in love, declaring himself, and having advanced to a stage requiring new undergarments. What is wrong with him? they demand. Diagnoses follow, ranging from asexual to homosexual. It is all, in its own way, adorable — their loyalty and their high opinion of the widow Lipman. I call these women my pit crew. I'll call him John Doe.

Coitus nonexistus is hard on one's women friends. When we gather, the topic of my non–love life almost always comes up. When I count how many friends and correspondents weigh in on the nomance, I come up with approximately two dozen, including my agent, my brother-in-law, and my day doorman. I tell them that you shouldn't judge or hate someone you've never met.

I also ask this: If I continue to "see" him in unsentimental but fond fashion — museums, movies, and dinners mostly — why do they have to weigh in? Once, over a solo dinner with Ben, when I thought the nomance might be taking a turn toward the mildly romantic, my otherwise self-assured and rarely self-conscious son averted his eyes and asked, as if in pain, "Does he kiss you good night?"

I said yes.

Pause. Then, barely audible, "On the lips?"

I said yes.

So how am I taking all this? I seem to be enjoying myself. I held a contest for my most fiercely oppositional friends, who happen all to be writers. I told them I was signing a book for John Doe, the only one of mine he hadn't read, so please send me their suggestions on how I should inscribe it, adding, "I'm laughing already," lest they take the assignment seriously.

The winner, Liz (again, never met him), wrote:

Dear Douchebag,
   Next time, BUY THE BOOK.
   Love,
   No, sorry, Like,
   Oops, sorry sorry I mean, Your FRIEND,
   Elinor.
   p.s. you're gay.

I wrote to the other contestants, "We have a winner!" and to Liz: "FOTFL" (fall on the floor laughing). I can't explain my own merriment in this matter, except to say that I appreciate funny writing and that, as another friend observed, my default setting is cheerful. Most of the pit crew say things like, "We just don't want you to be hurt," to which I answer, "Bob had a terrible fatal disease, and then he died. Did I fall apart?"

"No," they say.

I ask, "Do you think I'm going to fall apart if John Doe doesn't want to see me ever again?"

"As long as you're not holding out any hope," they say.

"As long as he's not taking up too much of your time," say my son and several others.

"Name the things you like about him," Liz demanded over dinner one night. I told her that we'd watched the returns of the 2012 New Hampshire primary together. "What other

Democrat is as interested in Republican primaries and debates as he is? No one. So I'd say the political stuff is right up there on my list. Who else is going to watch those with me?"

Liz protested, "All of your friends are! Every single one of us."

I said, "But I asked you to come over and watch the returns with me, and you didn't answer."

"Oh," she said. "Sorry."

Of course when they ask what is the latest with the nomance, I could say, "No comment" or "None of your business" or "I'd rather not talk about Mr. Doe." But I don't want to be rude. I love my friends. I've made it their vicarious business and given them their front-row seats. When I told my BFF early one evening that Doe was coming over to watch the next set of primary returns in approximately an hour, she said I must never be afraid of telling her anything. That she wants to know all. That she supports me and would never judge.

I laughed because what she kindly and supportively and generously wouldn't ever judge was my seeing a man approximately once a week in a state of declared platonicism.

Three years after Bob died, I've discovered this about myself: that I don't like too much attention. I canceled a second date with an online fellow because he called; e-mailed; bought me cookies, bagels, and cream cheese; downloaded samples of six of my novels between our introductory telephone conversation and our lunch date; and e-mailed me the morning of the lunch date to say it was cold out and I should bundle up.

Upon hearing how such thoughtfulness was off-putting,

BFF asked me if Bob used to bring me flowers and that sort of thing. I said hardly ever — just the first Valentine's Day of our courtship in 1972 and then again in 2006.

"See," she said. "You're not used to it. And I don't think you even like it."

When I ran this by my sister, she agreed. Then added rather confidently, "And you're not sentimental."

Oh, dear. I countered with, "Except over Ben?"

She granted me that. She is an organizational consultant and is good at analyzing human dynamics. After spending a weekend with me and witnessing some antiplatonicism, she dubbed the naysayers "The Mean Girls" (average age, fifty-two). She says my self-esteem is higher than theirs. Unlike me, they would need attention, reinforcement, and real dates as opposed to appointments.

It's my own fault, my own big mouth. Too much sharing. Consequently, my friends are divided into what I call the Yes Team and the No Team. One friend, an otherwise very nice woman, likes to say, "He's playing you! He's a player!"

I say, "There's only one thing missing — the playing."

The cocaptains of the No Team — their station and rank unknown to them — earned their title this way: One said that the roses John Doe once brought me were the wrong color. I didn't even ask what the right color would have been. The other often tells me that I must not ever turn down an invitation (she means from her) because I'm waiting for John Doe to call. The last time she said this (for at least the fourth time), I leaned forward in my chair and said, "That's a good lesson for teenage girls in high school who are waiting around for a boy to call. But I'm sixty-one years old. I'm a widow. If I goddamn want to wait for someone to get back to me about an invitation I issued, I will."

I am learning how judgmental and outspoken people are, more than I had occasion to experience in earlier social and marital chapters of my life. No one took much interest in the tone and frequency of Bob's romancing me — not about where we went, how often, and who paid. But now, as a single woman who's been a little too free with the paper trail of e-vites and thank-yous, out comes the microscope, the advice, and the heckling. I was indulgent up to a point, then the friendships suffered. Another lesson learned: pessimism and mistrust lie with their conveyors. "We don't see things as they are," Anaïs Nin once said. "We see them as *we* are."

The Yes Team members earned their place by saying things such as, "Having a real friend and intellectual soulmate is a wonder, especially in a town where many relationships are shallow and/or fleeting." Another wrote, "You say 'friends without benefits'? Oh I think you two are friends with many benefits."

I said to my BFF, "Think of it this way: It's as if he sits behind me in algebra class. He likes me and I like him. We go out. We have fun."

"And once in a while he pulls your pigtail?" she asked.

"And once in a while he pulls my pigtail."

He has told me in word and in deed that we are not a romance. I take it too well because he is such good company. He is smart. I tease him, and I learn a lot from him.

My cousin Laura (Yes Team), who believes in all things airy-fairy, religious, and imaginary, asked me if I've heard of the law of attractions. I said, "Sure." She continued: "You are a classic example. You weren't looking for a boyfriend. You don't want a real romance. You've always said you don't want to get married again. You're not ready. And you know what? How can you complain? The signal you were putting out into the universe very clearly was *friend*. I know you don't believe in this stuff, but you got exactly what you were asking for."

I thought about this. Finally, I asked, "Chaste Dates?"

"Chaste Dates," she said.

Back in make-believe, my protagonist did find love and did get laid. Farther along on the social/widow continuum than I, Gwen-Laura Schmidt's time had come.